Introduc

C000281968

Every winter thousands of people attend evening classes organised by the Royal Yachting Association. Some students are hoping to obtain one of the RYA's formal qualifications. Others want to brush up their navigational theory before buying a cruising yacht – or maybe they just feel like a change from learning French.

Whatever the motivation, this book is aimed at those taking the Day Skipper course. And this new edition has been reworked to take full account of the revolution in navigational practice brought about by electronic equipment such as the Global Positioning system (GPS) – as it relates to this particular RYA training programme.

The book is still designed primarily as a 'crammer' – a concise but comprehensive guide to revising for, and of course, passing, the relevant assessments.

Although the RYA does not regard its shorebased courses as an examination process – it merely awards 'certificates of satisfactory completion' – students don't necessarily take such a relaxed view. To them, the exercises and assessment papers look decidedly like exams. Some have to be taken under invigilation – in this case one general paper and another on chartwork. So most people need to do a bit of 'cramming' the night before the test.

This book tries to help by looking for the logic as well as the facts, eliminating unnecessary information to concentrate on the essentials of the RYA syllabus. Each section – **nautical terms, pilotage and navigation, weather, passage planning, the rule of the road, safety** – attempts to do several things:

- Provide virtually all the essential information, assuming no prior knowledge.
- Organise it in a form that makes learning and revision easier – so you can skim through the book on the train home, or just before going into an exam.
- Set all this in a practical seagoing perspective.

The RYA training programme is a voluntary scheme (in co-operation with the Department of Transport) 'to encourage high standards of seamanship and

'Can you spare a minute, Skip?'

navigation among yachtsmen and women' and avoid unnecessary regulation. It operates at five levels: Competent Crew, Day Skipper/Watch Leader, Coastal Skipper, Yachtmaster Offshore, and Yachtmaster Ocean. There are approved courses covering all of these (plus diesel engine maintenance, radar and survival) with practical examinations for the last three leading to the award of 'certificates of competence'.

So the shorebased course we are concerned with here is a combined one, for **Day Skipper/Watch Leader** candidates, involving a minimum of 40 hours teaching plus work at home. The current syllabus is set out in the RYA's Cruising Logbook. Classroom tuition is a preparation – if required – for two practical courses, each lasting about five days, after which students should be able to skipper a small yacht in familiar waters by day (Day Skipper) or take charge of a watch on a sail training vessel (Watch Leader).

Pass Your Day Skipper should get you successfully under way.

To make things easier, we have used **bold** type and tinted panels and boxes to pick out key phrases and facts to help you with your revision.

The symbols at the bottom of each right hand page are to test your knowledge – the answers are overleaf.

Nautical terms

It might be encouraging – but quite unrealistic – to suggest that the nautical jargon which often bewilders newcomers to boating can somehow be avoided. At first, it may seem like affectation to ask someone, say, to 'harden in the jib sheet, so the clew's almost touching the forward shrouds'. But without the jargon words, the same request would be far more complicated – 'pull that rope attached to the triangular sail at the front of the boat until the back corner almost reaches the first of the vertical wires supporting the mast'.

The truth is that every sailor ends up using a strange esoteric language. And so will you. It works well at sea, and more to the point, the RYA expects potential Day Skippers to acquire a 'working knowledge' of nautical terminology.

The good news is there are no exam questions on this subject. You can pick up the nautical terms as you go along, perhaps by going down to a marina and comparing textbook diagrams with real boats. And fortunately, since English is already so full of nautical metaphor, you may find that far from *taking you aback*, this section of the course turns out to be *plain sailing*.

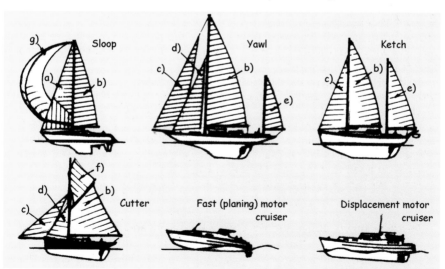

Types of boats. Key to labels: a) genoa, b) mainsail, c) jib, d) staysail, e) mizzen, f) topsail, g) spinnaker.

Parts of a boat

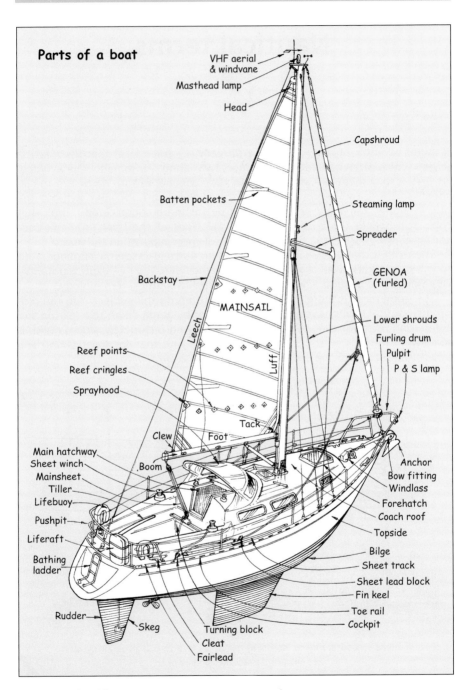

VHF aerial & windvane
Masthead lamp
Head
Capshroud
Batten pockets
Steaming lamp
Spreader
GENOA (furled)
Backstay
MAINSAIL
Lower shrouds
Furling drum
Pulpit
P & S lamp
Leech
Luff
Reef points
Reef cringles
Sprayhood
Tack
Clew   Foot
Main hatchway
Sheet winch
Mainsheet
Tiller
Lifebuoy
Pushpit
Liferaft
Bathing ladder
Boom
Anchor
Bow fitting
Windlass
Forehatch
Coach roof
Topside
Bilge
Sheet track
Sheet lead block
Fin keel
Toe rail
Cockpit
Rudder
Skeg
Turning block
Cleat
Fairlead

North cardinal buoy

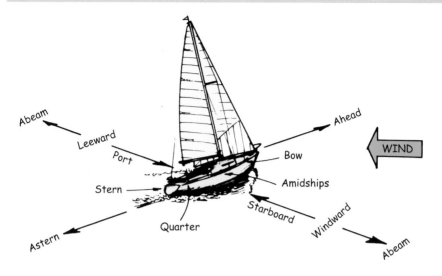

Terms describing position.

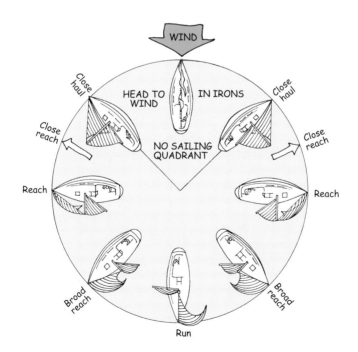

Points of sailing.

Navigation

Electronic Navigation

Yacht navigation has been transformed over the past decade or so by the availability of cheap, reliable electonic equipment – especially the **Global Positioning System (GPS)**. Before discussing various aspects of navigation in detail, therefore, it is worth looking at this technological revolution in broad outline – and at the way the RYA's Day Skipper training syllabus has responded.

The good news is that accurate navigation is now much easier. The downside (really no more than a strong note of caution) is that GPS does not solve all our navigational problems. As we come to rely on it, it is doubly important to have some sort of back-up, based on traditional methods.

The reality of modern yacht navigation is that once a boat is fitted with GPS, this almost inevitably becomes the primary method of position fixing. The compass, formerly used for this purpose, serves merely to steer a course.

The RYA now acknowledges this by assuming – at least for the purpose of its Day Skipper courses – that every yacht is fitted with GPS, and that its students will normally navigate by this method. But of course even the most robust and reliable electronic equipment can fail, perhaps just when you need it most. A flat battery will leave it useless. Quite rightly, therefore, RYA instructors still treat GPS as a powerful aid to navigation, not a complete substitute for traditional methods. Some non-electronic back-up is essential.

GPS – benefits and limitations

GPS is a satellite-based system which calculates a yacht's position to within a few metres, and constantly updates that position. This information can either be tranferred to a nautical map – a paper chart – or integrated with an electronic chart display. In other words it tells you where you are and how you got there.

What it does *not* do is solve the other half of the navigational problem – how to get *safely* from where you are now, to the destination you want to reach. To give an exaggerated example, suppose your yacht was off the south coast of Devon and you intended to sail round Land's End to some specified

Position line

harbour on the north Devon coast. In answer to the simple question: What course do I steer to reach that harbour?, the GPS would invite you to sail north, straight across Dartmoor.

A GPS set would nevertheless be immensely helpful on this West Country trip. Knowing precisely where you are at any moment, especially at night, or in fog, is half the problem. A simple electronic display would also guide your boat to intermediate 'waypoints', plotted by you, around the coast of Land's End.

But the underlying point is that, miraculous though GPS may seem – and even assuming it never breaks down – making proper use of it requires intelligent human intervention. The basic principles of navigation still have to be understood, and that is what the Day Skipper syllabus ensures.

Charts

Whatever your navigational method, you will not get far without a **chart** – a map giving more information about water than land. It enables you to record your position and plot a course to your destination.

Modern charts can take the form of an electronic display attached to the GPS, and the RYA's instructional pack will include a CD-ROM incorporating a practice chart, that can be projected in the classroom or used in your personal laptop. But you will start by using a chart in its age-old form, printed on stiff paper and spread out on a table.

It shows the **depth** of water and warns of obstacles along the way, such as **rocks** or **sandbanks**. Navigational **buoys** and **lighthouses** are marked on it to confirm your changing position. And to make best use of it – independent of GPS – the boat needs not just a **compass**, but also a **log** for measuring speed and distance, and an **echo sounder** to indicate the depth of water.

The navigator on an offshore racing yacht is always poring over the chart table, maintaining an accurate plot. Your coastal cruising man can sometimes make do with a folded chart stuffed into a plastic cover, provided he antici-pates the occasions when he really *does* need an accurate position – approaching a dangerous coastline, or feeling his way through shallow sandbanks on a falling tide. Different circumstances call for different methods. And for the time being, we are still in the classroom preparing for an exam.

The RYA's instructional notes make the same point: 'At sea it is often imprac-ticable or even undesirable to work to high levels of precision, but at times the safety of the yacht depends on precise navigation and accurate calculations. The course exercises assume the latter and the questions require a navigational precision of 0.1 mile and 0.1 metre for tidal calculations.'

This does not mean, however, that your navigational exercises will be full of complex arithmetic. On the contrary, the aim of this course is simply to establish the basic concepts. The examples chosen for exercises or exams are quite straightforward.

There are many ways of describing a boat's position, for example by reference to the direction and distance of a coastal landmark. The most fundamental method – and the basis of most charts – is to define her position on the Earth's surface in degrees north or south of the Equator (**latitude**), and east or west of the Greenwich meridian (**longitude**). Horizontal lines of latitude, from 0–90°, are parallel to one another, and sometimes referred to simply as parallels; whereas lines of longitude, or meridians, measured from 0–180°, converge at the North and South Poles.

So parallels and meridians are angular measurements along the circumference of the globe numbered in degrees, minutes (sixtieths of a degree), and tenths of a minute. Britain, for example, lies between latitudes 50° and 60°N of the Equator, and between longitudes 2°E and 15°W of Greenwich. If you wanted to pinpoint London's Tower Bridge on the globe, you could say it was at **51° 30'.3 N, 0° 04'.5 W**, and use this information to locate it on any map which has degrees of latitude and longitude marked along its edges – which marine charts always do. In fact they are covered with a grid of lines to make plotting the lat and long easier.

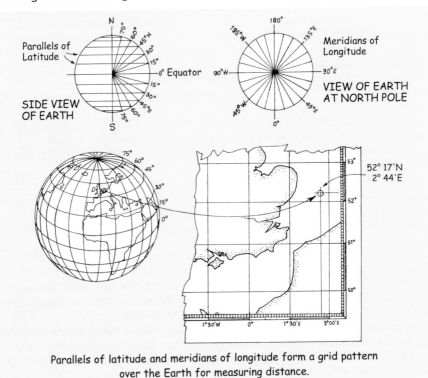

Parallels of latitude and meridians of longitude form a grid pattern
over the Earth for measuring distance.

Major light

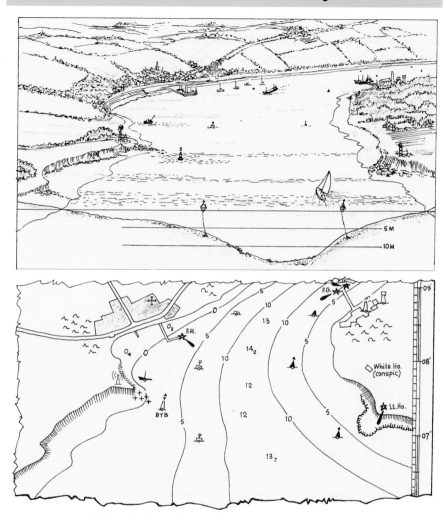

What the chart shows – think of it as a nautical map.

Charts, like land maps, are a projection of the Earth's curved surface on to a flat sheet of paper. The common projection is **Mercator's**. This spreads out lines of longitude so they appear parallel instead of converging at the North Pole as they do on a globe. But to avoid distorting the shape of the coastline, lines of latitude also have to be proportionately further apart as you move north.

One minute of latitude is a **nautical mile**, averaging out (the Earth itself is not exactly spherical) at 1852 metres. But a mile will *look* longer at the top of a

Mercator chart than at the bottom. And an important practical implication of this, when we come to it, is that **distances should always be measured from the latitude scale along the side of the chart, roughly level with the yacht's position**.

One odd result of Mercator projection is that a straight line on the chart is not the shortest distance between two real points. Although this rarely matters to yachtsmen, some other charts use a **Gnomonic projection**, showing the meridians converging as they would on a globe. On an ocean crossing, the direct course can then conveniently be drawn straight.

British charts are based on underwater surveys commissioned by the UK Hydrographic Office (UKHO), supplemented by information from equivalent organisations abroad, and marketed as Admiralty charts. This comprehensive series (also available in electronic or Raster form for most parts of the world) sets the standard. However Admiralty charts are designed primarily for use on the full-sized chart table of a warship, or a large merchant ship. So to match those published specially for yachtsmen by Imray and Stanfords, the UKHO has recently produced *Small Craft Folios*, and the folded *Small Craft Editions*.

Everyone will have their own preference amongst these yachting charts, but if necessary they can all be stuffed into a transparent waterproof cover and taken out into a wet cockpit. They also provide valuable supplementary information, such as harbour plans and tidal stream charts, presented from the perspective of a small boat rather than a 100,000 ton tanker.

Having selected a chart, you need to know whether it is up to date. Small changes are frequent and often important. Finding a buoy in the 'wrong' position – or just not there at all – can be thoroughly disconcerting.

On Admiralty charts, the **date of the edition** is shown in the margin with a reference to corrections in the weekly *Notices to Mariners*. Imray give the edition date and attach a list of corrections. Stanfords give the edition and the date to which each chart is corrected. All of these publishers supply subsequent corrections on their respective websites, or by post.

The traditional **unit of depth** at sea is the fathom – 6 feet. Some charts, particularly in America, still use this notation. However nearly all European charts now mark minimum depths in metres and tenths of a metre, so on the Day Skipper course you need only think metric. The chart shows both spot depths and depth contours, to convey the general shape of the seabed. Where numbers are underlined, they indicate the **drying height** above low water. (See also the chart extract given in the colour section at the centre of the book.)

There are hundreds of other **symbols** and **abbreviations**, listed as *Admiralty Chart No 5011* (which is actually a booklet) but many are self explanatory – like the little drawings of buoys with their distinctive topmarks.

Many students will be content simply to note common symbols as they occur, but if you want to learn them systematically, some categories are obviously more important – ways of marking wrecks and dangerous rocks, for example, and light characteristics (see page 26).

Observed position or fix

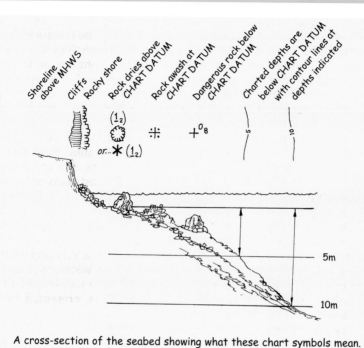

A cross-section of the seabed showing what these chart symbols mean.

On a metric chart, a lighthouse might be annotated Fl(2) 10s 28m 20M + F.WRG.14m 17–13M. This would mean:

- The main light flashes twice every 10 seconds.
- It stands 28 metres above high water on a spring tide.
- The light's luminous range is 20 miles (beware possible confusion between lower case m for metres and upper case M for miles).
- The lower, 14 metre light has three fixed sectors: white, red and green which are visible from 17–13 miles.

The **sectors** of the fixed light show different colours across different areas – perhaps a shallow coastline (green), a deeper channel (white), and a dangerous shoal (red).

The **luminous range** is the distance from which it can be seen in clear visibility – not necessarily the same as the **geographical range**, which is the distance at which a light shows above the horizon if your eye level is 15 feet above the water (on the deck of an old sailing ship, for example). In practice, the 'loom' of a powerful lighthouse is often visible from seaward before the actual light rises above the horizon – a fascinating transition you can use to fix your position, as we shall see later.

R

Electronic charts

All this information can be transferred to the screen of a **chart plotter**, on which positions from the GPS are superimposed. There are two methods. To produce a **Raster** chart, the original data is simply photographed with a digital camera. For a **Vector** chart, the plotter is directly programmed. This is a more flexible technique in which, for example, data can be edited to suit the scale of the chart. Some Charting programmes can also take tidal streams into account.

Using the Vector system it is now permissible for a merchant ship to go to sea with no paper charts as back-up. But this is certainly not recommended on a yacht.

Compasses

The first primitive magnetic compass appeared in Europe at least 800 years ago. It pointed north, to the magnetic pole.

A full compass rose is marked with 32 points, each measuring 11¼° of the circle. But a yacht's **steering compass** usually shows just four, or maybe eight points – N, NE, E, SE and so on. The primary marking is in degrees from 0 to 360, probably at intervals of 5°. This is about the nearest you can steer a sailing boat at sea (although on the chart you plot a course to the nearest degree). The course is held by keeping a fore-and-aft 'lubber line' against the required mark on the compass card, or by setting a revolving grid on top of the compass card to the chosen course and then lining up the compass needle – and hence the boat. At night, the compass obviously needs some sort of illumination.

A small **hand bearing compass**, as its name suggests, is designed for taking bearings (ie the angular distance from N, in degrees from 0 to 360) of navigational marks such as buoys, headlands and lighthouses, so as to fix the yacht's position. There are many different designs, all based on some sort of sighting device against which the revolving compass card can easily be read.

A steering compass can be mounted in a variety of ways, to suit the particular boat. The important thing is to position it as far as possible from the magnetic interference of ferrous metals – eg an iron keel – and electrical equipment. Yet however much care is taken, the compass needle is almost bound to show some **deviation** from the Earth's magnetic pole, if only by a few degrees E or W.

A big deviation can be roughly checked by comparison with a hand bearing compass held well away from any interference. But deviation varies continuously with the boat's heading, so precise navigation requires a **deviation card** showing the error in degrees E or W for every couple of compass points, or better still a curve on which the error on any given course can be interpolated. To prepare an accurate card, turn your boat slowly through successive headings while checking the steering compass against the known bearing of a distant object – or build up a card as opportunities arise during the season. Look out for transits, because they make it easier. In practice, even a substantial error may not matter on a short coastal trip, but it certainly will on a long sea crossing.

Port hand buoy

Applying variation

Back in the Day Skipper classroom, though the problem of deviation needs to be understood, it does not feature in the exam questions. However, compass work also involves a more basic allowance – for the **variation** between the direction of the magnetic pole and true north as shown by the lines of longitude – and you must know how to apply it.

The **compass rose** printed on a chart is usually in fact two roses, one inside the other, providing both true and magnetic bearings from which a course can be plotted. In our part of the world, a compass needle points slightly west of true north. In the southern North Sea, for example, the present variation is about 3°W and slowly decreasing.

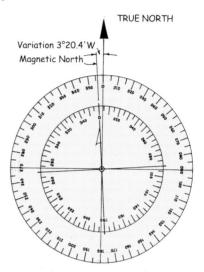

The compass rose.

You could navigate entirely with **magnetic** bearings and courses. Information from the yacht's compasses is, after all, in this form. But the chart grid is laid out on a **true** basis, with north at the top, and much of the other information you may need – for example tidal streams – is presented in the same form. So whatever you start with, the problem of **converting from magnetic bearings to true and vice versa** is going to arise – and in navigational exercises it arises only too often. So it is most important to understand and memorise the procedure for doing this.

Look at a double compass rose, and notice that with 3° westerly variation, a magnetic bearing is always that many degrees more than its true equivalent. True north lines up with 3° magnetic (0T=3M); true south lines up with 183° magnetic (180T=183M) and so on.

The same principle would apply if the compass difference was a combination of westerly variation and westerly deviation – say 3° variation and 4° deviation – a total of 7°W to be subtracted from the compass bearing (which, because of its deviation error, is no longer the same as the magnetic bearing) to make it true. True south would now line up with 187° on the compass (180T=187C).

On the other hand if the compass error is to the east – say an easterly deviation of 5° offset by 3° westerly variation, leaving a net error of 2°E – then the opposite rule will apply. The 2°E must be added to convert a compass reading to true, or of course subtracted to convert the other way.

If at first this all looks very confusing, don't worry. At sea it is usually much simpler. For any given area, variation can be treated as constant. Deviation varies

fS.M.Sh

with the boat's heading, but when it matters, there is usually time to put it right. In classroom exercises, you will only be expected to apply variation.

There are various sayings and mnemonics to help remember how it works, eg '**Variation West, Compass Best**', or '**ADDECT**' (**ADD** Easterly **C**ompass to **T**rue). Your instructor will no doubt suggest others – unless of course you prefer to work it out from first principles each time.

Measuring direction and distance

On leaving harbour – or any other known position on the chart, such as a navigational buoy – it is the navigator's job to tell the helmsman what compass course to steer.

The yacht could be heading directly for another harbour across open water, or for some intermediate position before turning on to a different course. In either case, the navigator usually starts by ruling a line on his chart, joining the two points. Any ruler would do for this purpose, but the traditional navigator's tool is the **parallel rule** (two rulers loosely linked together so they are always parallel). Having drawn the line, he can transfer its alignment to the nearest compass rose by 'walking' the parallel rule across the chart until it cuts the centre of the rose. Reading off the angle indicated on the inner, magnetic rose (and adjusting it for deviation) he finds the course to steer by keeping the compass's lubber line on the required number of degrees. He also labels the line on his chart. Nowadays many people prefer to use some form of 'plotter'

with its own handy compass rose (a plastic instrument not to be confused with an electronic chart plotter). You lay the edge of the plotter on the course line and swivel the compass rose to line up with the chart grid, making sure that north is up. Then read the course or bearing where the mark shows you.

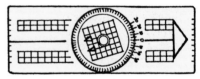

A course plotter.

Next, you calculate the distance between the two points to estimate the time of arrival, course change, or whatever. Opening a pair of one-handed **dividers** to span the plotted course, you transfer them to the **side of the chart** – never the top or bottom, for the reasons explained above – and measure off the number of nautical miles (ie minutes of latitude) opposite the yacht's position.

And remember that the direct magnetic **course** steered to reach a given destination – say, a navigational buoy – is also the compass **bearing** of that buoy. Such bearings are the common raw material of pilotage and navigation.

The distance a yacht moves through the water (not necessarily the same as distance over the ground, because of the tides) is measured by a **log**. As the name suggests, this was originally a wooden log thrown over the stern on a line,

Fine sand with mud and shells

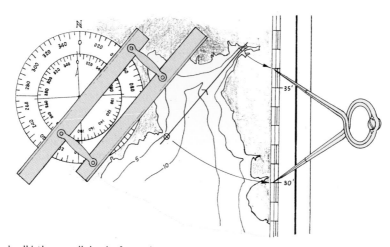

You 'walk' the parallel rule from the position line to the compass rose and read off the angle to give your course or bearing. Use the dividers to span the course, then read off the distance from the latitude scale.

to see how fast the knots marking the line ran out (hence also the nautical term **'knots', meaning nautical miles per hour**). Nowadays it exists in many forms – towed (mechanical or electrical), retractable hull-mounted, doppler or ultrasonic – each with its pros and cons. A log measuring speed through the water also estimates the distance covered, because one largely determines the other. But a navigator ultimately wants to know the distance – so as to calculate his position, and on a long sea crossing, when he should start looking for a landfall.

The other measurement which always concerns a coastal navigator is the **depth of water** under his keel, both to avoid running aground and to find his position on the chart. The traditional method of sounding shallow depths at sea is the **lead line** – a line marked in fathoms with strips of leather and bunting, attached to a lump of lead and 'armed' with sticky tallow. For routine depth measurement this has long since been replaced by the electronic echo sounder, but the lead is still a useful back-up: to 'feel' the uneven bottom round an anchorage – perhaps testing those chart symbols that describe the seabed as mud (M) or shingle (Sn) – and to calibrate your echo sounder.

An **echo sounder** works by measuring the time it takes for an ultrasonic pulse emitted by a hull-mounted 'transducer' to be reflected back from the seabed. There are four main types of display: digital, rotating LED (light emitting diode), dial, and trace – each with its advantages. Probably the simplest is the digital (numerical) display, in metres or feet. On a dial, the moving pointer gives a clear sense of changing depth, while the 'fishfinder'

trace shows the seabed contours. But the classic in this field is the rotating LED, which shows movement clearly and is easily visible at night, though it does require periodic adjustment to eliminate a secondary echo.

The echo sounder is invaluable in pilotage and navigation, especially when fitted with a depth alarm. The alarm can be set to warn of dangerously shallow water, to signal the presence of a deep trough in the seabed, or help the navigator to follow a depth contour in bad visibility.

Tides

Unlikely as it might seem, tides are produced by the gravitational pull of the moon and, to a lesser extent, the sun. The orbiting moon produces two high tides every day, or to be a little more precise, in a period of about 24 hours 50 minutes – which is why the time of high water (HW) is about 50 minutes later each day.

When the moon is full, or new, the sun's gravitational pull is exerted in the same direction. The movement of water is greater, tidal streams run faster, the tides rise higher – and fall lower – than at other times, oscillating about their **mean level (ML)**. Such **spring tides** occur every fortnight, in keeping with the phases of the moon. At any given place on the coast, this also means that **high water springs (HWS)** is always at roughly the same time of day.

In alternate weeks, when the sun is pulling at right angles to the moon, the tidal range is smaller. These sluggish **neap tides** are less helpful in floating your boat out of a mud berth, but better for crossing a shallow bar at **low water (LW)** as we shall see later when planning a passage.

Depths marked on a chart are measured from a level known as the **chart datum** – either the **mean level** of **low water spring tides (MLWS)** or more commonly the level of the lowest astronomically predictable tide (**LAT**). The height of a tide is also measured from the chart datum, as is the height of a drying sandbank or rock. But note that a lighthouse is measured from **mean high water springs (MHWS)** – important, but easily forgotten, when calculating the distance at which the light is visible.

The primary source of **tidal predictions** is the *Admiralty Tide Tables*, Volume 1 of which covers British waters, although tide tables are also available in many local publications and in **nautical almanacs** produced for yachtsmen, such as *Reeds Nautical Almanac*. This contains information on a vast range of other subjects – navigation (including passage planning, GPS waypoints, tidal streams, pilotage and harbour charts), and other useful information. You can also buy tide table software programmes for your PC that will work out tidal times and heights.

Opening the Admiralty **tide tables** at the pages dealing with the 'standard port' of Dover, you will find the times and heights of high and low water laid out for each day of the year (times in Universal Time, heights in metres). Associated

Water track

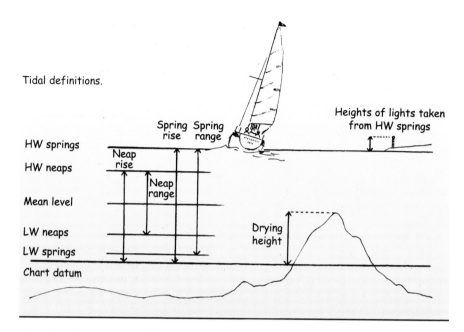

Tidal definitions.

with the table is a steeply humped **tidal curve**, or to be more precise, two curves superimposed: a solid line for springs, and a dashed line for neaps, with times before and after HW marked along its base. Curves like this are the basis of the Admiralty method of tide calculation you will use for Day Skipper exams.

Notice that tidal height is not marked directly in metres, but in proportional 'factors' ranging from zero (LW) to 1.0 (HW), because the 'shape' of the tide – that is the varying rate at which it flows in and out, as represented by the curve – is determined separately from its height. For example this particular curve shows that during the first hour of a spring flood, the water will rise by less than a tenth of its eventual range (a factor of less than 0.1); after four hours of an ebbing neap tide, the level will have fallen to about four tenths of the range (a factor of 0.4), and so on; the springs curve is noticeably skewed to the right, indicating that at Dover, these big tides flood for five hours and ebb for seven.

To translate factors into actual depths above chart datum, the predicted heights for a particular day are plotted as a sloping line to the left of the curve (using the horizontal scales provided), so that you can read across from one to the other.

Similar curves are published for each of the **standard ports.** Some are quite symmetrical, others sharply skewed. For ports in the Bristol Channel, where the tidal range is enormous, they are steeply peaked. In the North Sea – if drawn to the same scale – they are much flatter. Southampton provides the famous anomaly of a double peak at springs, ie a second high water, because of the complex way tides flow round the Isle of Wight.

Rule of Twelfths

Sometimes if you want a quicker approximation of height of tide, you can use a simple arithmetical process called the **Rule of Twelfths** which is based on the assumption that the tide rises or falls as follows:

In the **first** hour the tide rises **one twelfth** of its range
In the **second** hour the tide rises **two twelfths** of its range
In the **third** hour the tide rises **three twelfths** of its range
In the **fourth** hour the tide rises **three twelfths** of its range
In the **fifth** hour the tide rises **two twelfths** of its range
In the **sixth** hour the tide rises **one twelfth** of its range

The Rule of Twelfths is obviously less accurate than a tidal curve calculation, especially where the tidal range is large or the shape asymmetrical. But then these are by no means the only sources of error in tidal predictions. The actual height is always affected by atmospheric pressure, for example. A storm surge down the North Sea can raise tides by a metre or more above their predicted level – as happened in the disastrous 1953 floods. An incoming tide constricted by a long estuary may arrive in a great rush (the Severn bore is an extreme example) while the first of the ebb often seems to drain away with a speed that belies the Rule of Twelfths. So make your calculations, and then apply a generous safety margin – especially in rough seas on a falling tide.

Meanwhile, back in the classroom, you have to face an assessment paper which treats the tidal predictions as exact to a tenth of a metre, so you must get the **Admiralty method** clear in your mind:

To find the height of tide (at a standard port) **at a given time** between high and low water:

1 calculate how many hours before or after HW your given time is, and mark it along the base of the curves (A);
2 from this starting point, draw a line (A1) vertically to meet the appropriate curve (springs or neaps);
3 proceed horizontally to meet the sloping tide line (T1-T2) showing the relevant range on the required day (A2);
4 proceed vertically up (A3) or down, to read off the height at your given time.

Isophase light (Iso) – equal light and dark periods

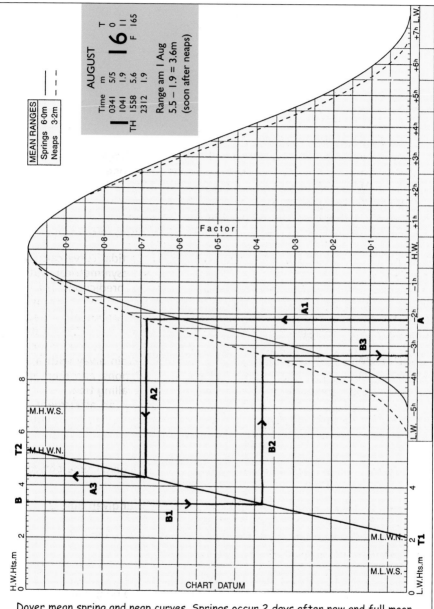

Dover mean spring and neap curves. Springs occur 2 days after new and full moon.
Extract from the *Admiralty Tide Tables Vol 1 NP 201-02*

'Relax! I told you she'd stop ranging about when the tide turned.'

East cardinal buoy

To find the time at which the tide will reach a given height ie the same calculation backwards:

1 starting from the required height on the horizontal height scale (B), draw a line vertically to meet the sloping tide line (B1);
2 proceed horizontally (B2) to the appropriate curve (springs or neaps, rising or falling);
3 proceed vertically down (B3) to read off the time before or after HW on the horizontal time scale.

In practice, of course, you will often be sailing on middling tides – neither springs nor neaps. If the two tidal curves for the nearest port are significantly different, check the actual range (HW–LW) against the ranges shown for springs and neaps, and then interpolate between them by eye.

Tidal curves for **secondary ports** are not normally available. Instead you must consult an almanac for time and height corrections to apply to the appropriate standard-port curve. Notice that corrections vary according to the time and height of the tide – in other words whether it is springs or neaps – so there may be more interpolating to be done, perhaps using a simple graph.

For yachtsmen based on the south coast of England, there is one final complication. Between Bournemouth and Selsey Bill, the shape of the tides is so grossly distorted that there may be a prolonged or double high tide which makes plotting heights difficult. Fortunately, low tide remains a single, clearly defined event, so tidal curves in this area are centred on LW. Where the shape of the spring and neap curves is widely different, a third 'critical' curve is also included, defined by reference to the range, to make interpolation easier.

Points to remember about tidal calculations

Where tidal calculations are concerned, the seamanlike rule is to match your method to the circumstances. Big tides mean big potential errors, so take extra care with your arithmetic. Easing into a muddy estuary on the flood, you can afford to run aground. Not so when crossing an exposed bar on the ebb – so allow a much bigger safety margin.

Tidal streams

You will find that information on tidal streams comes in two main forms – special little charts, often made up into a **tidal stream atlas**, and **tidal diamonds** on the main chart, which refer to a table of direction and speed.

On a set of chartlets (in an *Admiralty Tidal Stream Atlas*, in almanacs and on some charts – see chart extract in colour section) the streams at each hour before

Fl.G.3s
Name

and after HW at a particular port are shown by a pattern of arrows marked with the rate in knots at springs and neaps. The arrows vary in thickness according to the strength of the tide, so they give an excellent quick, general impression.

Tidal diamonds are diamond-shaped boxes, containing a letter, shown at useful places on the chart. They refer to tables showing the **rate and direction** at each hour (in case you come across the more traditional terms, the direction of a tide is sometimes referred to as the **set**, while the rate is the **drift**). This presentation is more convenient for chartwork because speed (the rate in knots) and direction (the true bearing along which the tide is flowing, not the direction it comes from, as with a wind) can be applied straight from the tables.

Points to remember about tidal streams

- They run stronger in deep water.
- They tend to set into bays and eddy round the back of headlands.
- In estuaries and narrow bottlenecks, or off major promontories, they can be accelerated into dangerous tide rips or races (charts refer to 'overfalls').

Before beginning to apply all this, there is one other basic source of which you should be aware – publications known as **sailing directions** or **pilots**. As their name suggests, they provide all the detailed local information needed to pilot a vessel through a particular stretch of water. The Admiralty publishes a comprehensive series traditionally famous for their little sketches of the coastline – now replaced by coloured photographs – and grim warnings to navigators. But yachtsmen may be better served by one of the many specialist pilot books covering various cruising areas.

Pilotage

Pilotage is largely visual navigation – the sort you need when first leaving harbour to explore the local coastline. The techniques are simple, but sometimes difficult to apply. Finding your way into a rock-strewn estuary, for example, may involve rapid changes of course with only a small margin for error. So you need some sort of pilotage plan, and **if your plan is at all complicated, write it down** – on a single sheet of paper in a plastic cover that you can take into the cockpit.

When 'buoy hopping' in bad weather or poor visibility, it is extremely helpful, when you reach each mark, to have pre-plotted the bearing and distance of the next. As the boat lurches round and the boom crashes over, you immediately know where to steer and where to look (something the GPS will also tell you, if the relevant waypoint has already been entered).

Light float

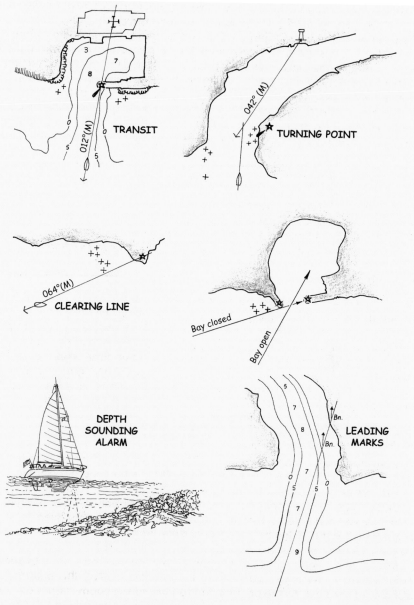

TRANSIT

TURNING POINT

CLEARING LINE

DEPTH SOUNDING ALARM

LEADING MARKS

Pilotage uses many visual aids and techniques to help you to navigate safely inshore.

RW

The hand bearing compass often plays its part, to establish **turning points** and/or **clearing lines** – the maximum or minimum bearings that will lead you clear of dangerous rocks or shoals. But when making your plan, **look first for transits** between a couple of prominent marks, because these give a bearing without reference to anything but your own eyes. Hence, of course, the value of purpose-built **leading marks** to bring vessels safely into harbour – the ultimate aid to pilotage.

If it is a commercial harbour, remember that big ships 'constrained by their draft' or otherwise disinclined to get out of your way, may be among the dangers to be avoided. Plot an approach that keeps you clear to one side of the deep water channel. And where relevant – for example a busy ferry port – consult an almanac to note the **harbour signals** controlling ships entering or leaving.

'It's very satisfactory when they turn up dead on the nose like the "West Knock" there.'

An echo sounder (preferably with an alarm) will help a lot, both to warn of shallow water and to indicate your position above the seabed's contours.

If there are **buoys** along your track, steer fairly close to them (unless of course they mark an isolated danger). In poor visibility, especially, you want to be doubly sure you have the correct one, by reading a name or a number. You then set off on the next course from a confirmed position (though not an absolutely precise one, because buoys must have a fair scope of mooring chain to cope with the tidal range). As you pass the buoy, the water swirling round it also acts as an excellent tidal stream indicator.

Safe water mark

The IALA buoyage system

Navigational buoys are distinguished by shape, colour, and the light they show. Their arrangement at sea follows **two main systems: lateral and cardinal**. (See diagram in colour section.)

In a lateral system, buoys are laid to port and starboard of the navigable water according to what is known as the conventional direction of buoyage – which runs from SW to NE round the British Isles and then into the various estuaries and rivers. This method lends itself to marking a clearly defined channel, especially in an estuary where the conventional direction leads into port with the flood tide.

In a cardinal system buoys are identified with the cardinal points of the compass: N, E, S, and W, and placed in that direction from the point of interest or danger they mark. This method is particularly suitable for marking the edges of a sandbank or a coastal reef, although cardinal buoys may also signal the entrance to a channel.

The **IALA System A** used in Europe (IALA is the International Association of Lighthouse Authorities) combines both lateral and cardinal principles – port and starboard marks for channels and cardinal ones mainly for other features.

Lateral marks

Lateral marks on the **port** side of a channel are **flat-topped can** or **pillar buoys**, while those to **starboard** are **conical** or **pointed**. They are coloured **red to port** and **green to starboard**, as are the lights they show – matching the colours of a ship's navigational sidelights. At night, therefore, it is the *colour* of a lateral buoy's light that conveys its basic message, rather than the light's rhythm, which varies merely to distinguish individual buoys.

Cardinal marks

Cardinal marks adopt the opposite approach, using the *rhythm* of the light – which is always white – as well as the buoy's shape and colour, to convey its message. These are tall black and yellow buoys with a distinguishing topmark formed by two black cones. The two cones of a **north** cardinal topmark both point up to the 'top' of the world (like the old fashioned gale warning cones) and those on a **south** cardinal buoy downwards.

Cones forming the **west** and **east** topmarks point in opposite directions, and yachtsmen often remember them by their resemblance to a **W**ineglass and an **E**gg respectively. The black and yellow bands on the buoy's structure (see diagram in colour section) have a similar logic, though watch out for rust and seaweed which can sometimes obscure the pattern.

Light characteristics

These are arranged rather like a clock face – continuous single flashing for north, a group of three flashes for east at 'three o'clock', six for south (plus a distinguishing long flash) and nine for west. The shorter flashes can be either 'quick' (about once a second) or 'very quick' (twice a second).

An **occulting light** remains lit most of the time, with only short periods of darkness – in other words the reverse of flashing. The adjective **isophase** (compare isobar) means that periods of light and dark are equal. Notice that these last two characteristics are both associated with safety, whereas the double white flash of a black and red buoy marking an isolated danger, and carrying two black spheres, conveys the opposite message.

'Is it supposed to remind you of an egg cup... keep to the East, or a wine glass... keep to the West?'

Wreck visible at low water

Light symbol abbreviations

G	green
W	white
F	fixed (steady light)
Fl	single flashing
L Fl	long flashing (at least 2 seconds)
Fl(3)	group flashing (groups of 3)
Q	continuous quick flashing
Q(3)	groups of 3 quick flashes
IQ	interrupted quick flashing
VQ	continuous very quick flashing
VQ(3)	groups of 3 very quick flashes
IVQ	interrupted very quick flashing
Oc	occulting (only short periods of darkness)
Iso	isophase (equal periods of dark and lightness)

Chartwork

As the land recedes and visual references become fewer, it becomes increasingly important to plot the yacht's progress across the chart. To practise this sort of navigation you will need some equipment:

- A long ruler (preferably made of transparent plastic)
- A parallel rule for transferring bearings from a compass rose to another part of the chart (the roller kind are fine in the classroom but not on a yacht)
- And/or a course plotter such as the Portland, the Breton, or the Douglas protractor, some of which also make it easier to cope with compass deviation (your instructor will probably recommend one)
- A pair of one-handed dividers for measuring distance (avoid the sharply pointed models)
- A pair of drawing compasses for describing arcs
- A couple of soft hexagonal pencils and a big soft rubber (hard pencils or a small harsh rubber will destroy the surface on frequently used areas of the chart)

Symbols you will need to know are:

+	**dead reckoning (DR)**
△	**estimated position (EP)**
⊙	**observed position or fix** (position obtained from position lines)
→—	**water track** (wake course, allowing for leeway)
→→—	**ground track** (course made good relative to land)

>>> tidal stream
→ position line
«→» transferred position line
GPS waypoint (WP)

Most of the problems you will confront on the Day Skipper practice chart are variants of three basic geometrical calculations – fixing the yacht's position; plotting a compass course to reach a required position, and estimating your position after steering a given course for a certain distance. In its simplest form, this last calculation is known as **dead reckoning**. It makes no allowance for the tidal streams and leeway we shall discuss later. When you do make these allowances, the result is an **estimated position**.

Position fixing

In principle, any fix requires at least **two position lines**. These are lines along which the yacht's position must lie, so that if they intersect (and they are accurate) there is only one place she can be.

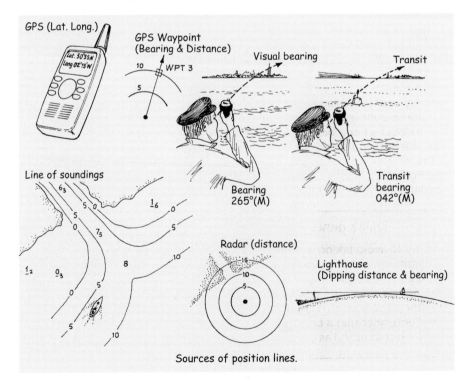

Sources of position lines.

Eddies

The **GPS** does this instantly by numerically displaying the lines of latitude and longitude which define your position on the globe. It will also give the bearing of a given waypoint, and provide a second position line – in the form of a circle – by calculating your distance from it. But there are many other sources of position lines that can be combined to confirm or substitute for this electronic information:

- A **hand compass bearing** of a visible object marked on the chart – a buoy, a light, or a 'conspic' tower.
- An extended line of **transit** between two visible objects.
- The **distance off** a coastline (radar does this well).
- The **dipping distance** of a lighthouse at night (ie the distance at which it dips below your horizon).
- A **line of depth soundings** (or just a single sounding if it establishes a position on a clearly defined seabed contour).

In an emergency only, the Coastguard might provide another position line by telling you the bearing of your VHF transmission.

Visual fixes

The simplest form of position line is a **transit** – the visual alignment of two charted objects, such as a lighthouse, a beacon, or a navigational buoy. Draw one line on the chart, without even referring to the compass rose, and you are half way to establishing your position. And if the two transit objects are a pair of purpose-built **leading marks** or **leading lights**, to indicate the safe approach to a harbour or the best water over a shallow bar, there is no need even to draw the line; you just follow them.

The commonest form of visual fix consists of two or more bearings, ie readings from a hand bearing compass, transferred to the chart with your parallel rule or plotter by reference to the compass rose.

Three general points to remember about fixes

- Try to avoid taking bearings from hills or headlands, because although they may look clearcut from seaward, locating their outline precisely on a two-dimensional chart may be difficult.
- Avoid shallow (acute or obtuse) angles between bearings because they increase the margin of error.
- Remember that a **back bearing** of something you have passed may be just as useful as one sighted ahead.

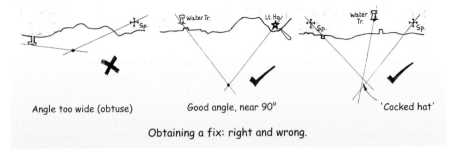

Angle too wide (obtuse)   Good angle, near 90°   'Cocked hat'

Obtaining a fix: right and wrong.

Fixing a position from three bearings should reduce the margin of error, but since sightings from a small yacht can never be absolutely precise, you will almost certainly be left with a triangular '**cocked hat**' on the chart. Your boat is probably in the middle of it, but if the position is critical, assume the worst case – or take some fresh bearings!

Even when only one charted object can be identified, it may be possible to establish a **running fix**, by taking two successive bearings. The first is plotted as a position line, along with the log mileage at that time. After a convenient interval you take a second bearing of the same object, and the course made good during the interval is plotted from any point on the first position line. This first line is then transferred so as to mark the only point on the second line where the track made good actually fits between the two bearings. That must be the yacht's position.

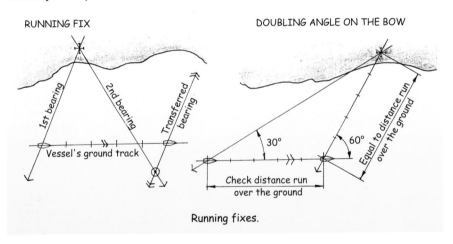

RUNNING FIX   DOUBLING ANGLE ON THE BOW

Running fixes.

Another sort of running fix involves **doubling the angle on the bow**. If you take a bearing of an object on the shore ahead and then maintain a steady course until the angle between bearing and course has doubled, the three lines plotted on the chart form a triangle with two equal sides. Using the log and a

Position of tabulated tidal stream

tidal atlas, we can calculate the length of one of those sides – the distance the yacht has covered – and that is also the distance off. So now you have two position lines to make a fix.

Yet another navigational dodge big ships used before the days of radar, and which can still be useful aboard a yacht, is to **combine the bearing of a light-house at night with its dipping distance**. The curvature of the Earth makes distant objects fall below the horizon with surprising speed. And the distance at which this happens to a lighthouse of a given height (plus the observer's own height above sea level) can be found from tables in nautical almanacs. The resulting position line is a circle round the light whose radius is that total distance. A compass bearing of the light, intersecting the circle, gives a fix (but remember the charted height of a lighthouse is measured from MHWS, so if it is not high water you must add on the difference between that and the actual tidal level before consulting the distance table).

Electronic fixes

The **Global Positioning System (GPS)** displays a constantly updated read-out of a yacht's position (in latitude and longitude) to an accuracy of a few metres.

This navigational magic is worked by analysing coded signals from a network of US military satellites orbiting the Earth. Provided with a series of positions, even the most modest GPS computer can instantly work out the yacht's course and speed over the ground, calculate the distance and bearing of any specified **waypoint (WP)** on the chart, and if required, the amount by which a yacht deviates from the direct track towards it.

Nowadays it is assumed that a yacht's position will normally be fixed by GPS. If you go on to take the Day Skipper practical course, you will also be expected to programme a waypoint into a simple GPS set, and follow the track towards it – nothing complicated.

The waypoint's position is entered in the GPS memory by its Lat and Long. and given a name – rather like storing telephone numbers in a mobile phone. With a number of such points, whole routes can easily be pre-programmed, leading the navigator from one nautical milestone to another. As we have already seen, more elaborate equipment includes an electronic chart plotter, displaying the boat's changing position. If called upon, it will relay that information automatically to the rescue services ashore (see Safety – (GMDSS).

Would-be skippers are shown how to use a chart plotter. But to make best use of GPS with a conventional paper chart, it is important not to treat this marvellous device as an entirely separate method of navigation. In principle, as explained above, it is a source of the navigator's vital position lines, like the hand bearing compass or the echo sounder. The numerical GPS read-out of Lat and Long, for instance, is not strictly a fix, merely an instruction for plotting two position lines which then provide the fix.

A waypoint is also a valuable source of position lines, as well as an inter-mediate destination. In this second role, it can be placed quite arbitrarily, for instance at the centre of the chart's compass rose, so as to obtain a different pair of position lines from the GPS display – ie the waypoint's bearing and distance from the yacht. This may be quicker than plotting lat and long.

Points to remember when using GPS

- Never enter waypoints straight from a directory or pilot book without plotting them on the chart.
- GPS gives you the *direct* course to a waypoint, not necessarily the *safe* course – it doesn't notice rocks in the way and it doesn't allow for tidal streams.
- Make sure you have entered a waypoint's Lat and Long *correctly*, by checking that its bearing and distance match your estimated position.
- Don't plot a waypoint exactly at a buoy or beacon – you might collide with it!

Any navigator presented with a resource as capable as GPS might be tempted to believe it makes traditional methods redundant. It is easier to install than a VHF radio. Simple handheld sets resemble a mobile phone. But in truth this is just another electronic aid – albeit an immensely powerful one – which could be rendered useless by a flat battery.

Log keeping

Hence the importance, highlighted in the Day Skipper syllabus, of checking and independently confirming the GPS data, and keeping a navigational record to fall back on if the GPS fails. Traditionally, this record is kept in the **ship's 'log'** (not to be confused with the log showing speed and distance).

There are many other reasons for keeping a log – guarding against the sudden onset of fog, for example – and there are various types of log to suit different vessels. The log of a motor yacht might include a record of rpm, temperature, charging rate and fuel state that would not be needed aboard a sailing yacht. But whatever the boat, on a long passage its navigator needs some way of plotting his position, or reworking a doubtful calculation, from a basic record of time, course, speed, navigational marks and so on.

On a large vessel where the crew is organised into watches – each with a Watch Leader – the log also helps to inform the new watch what has been happening while they were below.

Cold front

Plotting a course

Navigation would be a lot easier if, when you wanted to go north over the ground, you simply had to steer due north by the boat's compass. It is rarely that simple. First we must allow for **variation** (and perhaps deviation). But a sailing boat with the wind ahead or on the beam will also be making **leeway** – ie moving slightly crabwise, perhaps 5° downwind of the direction her bows are pointing. And then she will be affected by the **tidal stream**.

So this is the procedure, illustrated in the diagram, for plotting the course made good over the ground, or ground track, after allowing for variation (deviation is ignored), leeway and tidal stream:

1 Subtract westerly **variation** to convert magnetic course (M) to true (T).
2 Lay off the resulting true course steered for an hour from the observed position A; apply **leeway** downwind and label the resulting **water track**.
3 Measure the log **distance** through the water against the adjacent latitude scale and mark it off to give position B. (See diagram, below left.)
4 Look up the direction and rate of the **tidal stream** during that hour and lay them off as a measured line or 'vector' from B, to establish the **estimated position** C.
5 Join A to C and label the line as an approximation of the yacht's **ground track**.

The accuracy of this estimated position depends on how carefully the helmsman maintains his course, making a correct allowance for leeway (which varies with the type of boat and the set of the sails), the accuracy of the log reading and the tidal stream predictions. With so many variables, small boat navigation is never an exact science.

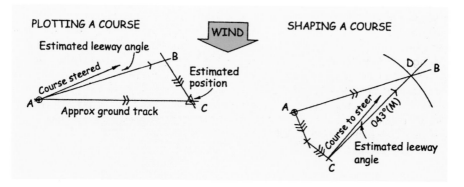

Shaping a course from a given position to reach another

In a sense this is the same triangular problem in reverse, anticipating the effect of tide and leeway instead of working it out afterwards. But notice an important difference: the yacht's progress is not measured from the starting point A, but from the end of the tidal vectors C. Note also that this diagram covers two hours with two successive vectors, because the tidal stream changes – a complication worth understanding here, though unlikely to crop up on your Day Skipper course. So here is the sequence:

1 Lay off the desired **ground track** from A to B. (See diagram page 33, right.)
2 Calculate roughly how long the trip will take (in this example something over two hours) and lay off the appropriate **tidal vectors** to point C.
3 With compasses set to the **distance** the yacht will cover during the same two hours, strike an arc from C through the desired ground track AB and mark it D, so that CD is the water track required to reach the nearest practical point to B.
4 Use a parallel rule or plotter to measure this **water track** against the magnetic compass rose and label it.
5 Apply an appropriate upwind correction for **leeway** (in an exercise this would be specified) to obtain the compass **course to steer**.

'We should be seeing land in precisely three and a quarter hours.'

Yacht harbour, marina

That's the theory, which for exercise purposes is all you need. But bear in mind that while the helmsman may steer a dead straight course from A to D, his yacht will actually follow a meandering curve over the ground. If you needed to stay close to the track from A to B – for example to avoid running aground – a separate course could be calculated for each hour's tidal stream. Otherwise, as here, the tidal vectors are plotted end to end to produce a single mean course to steer for the whole trip. As you near B, plot your estimated position and adjust the course to reach it exactly – or to be safe, aim a bit up-tide.

GPS, through its cross track function, is making similar calculations all the time, without knowing why. Having entered B as a waypoint, the size and direction of the **cross track error (XTE)** tells you what course correction to apply. But this is not a satisfactory substitute for the method described above.

How *carefully* you need to plot tidal vectors depends on the circumstances. On a short coastal trip the tide will either help or hinder progress; you just want to know by how much (a boat moving at 4½ knots with a 1½ knot tide under her travels twice as fast over the ground – 6 knots instead of 3 – as the same boat heading into the tide, which is why it is so important for small craft to work their tides). And there are other simple cases when a sideways ebb and flow will roughly cancel out, so that it may actually be more efficient to ignore the tidal stream.

But on any short trip with the tide across your bows, it pays to make positive allowance, if only by eye, or you could soon find yourself wildly off track. In light airs, a tidal stream may easily match the speed of a small sailing yacht.

Points to remember about navigation

- GPS is a superb source of position lines – until the battery goes flat or until the US military decide to reduce the signal accuracy for the public domain.
- Never miss an easy chance to fix your position visually eg from a transit.
- Measure distances along the side of the chart.
- Cardinal buoys follow the clock face, lateral ones match your navigation lights.
- 'Variation West, Compass Best'.
- Don't waste a favourable tide – even if it means getting up early.
- The Rule of Twelfths – 1,2,3,3,2,1.
- Pilotage usually involves rapid changes of course – prepare a written plan.
- Adapt your navigation to the circumstances eg falling tide or doubtful visibility.

Weather

Whether they admit it or not, students start this section of the course with one big advantage. Thanks to our obsession with the changeable British weather, much of the meteorologists' technical jargon is already familiar from newspaper forecast maps, and above all from radio and television. The BBC shipping forecast, with its mesmeric recital of wind strengths and directions, is almost a national institution. On TV, the weather presenters point out the close-packed 'isobars' which warn of gales, and show us satellite pictures of the swirling clouds that mark an advancing 'depression'. With this background, the meteorology syllabus is simply a matter of grasping a few basic patterns, definitions, and sources of information.

Fix

The weather system

At sea, yachtsmen are usually more interested in the wind strength and direction than whether it is wet or dry, hot or cold. But in truth it is temperature, the interaction of warm and cold air masses, that determines everything else.

In the British Isles we live more or less on a turbulent boundary – the 'polar front' – between the cold air of the polar regions and the warm air of the tropics. It is turbulent because the density of air, and very importantly the amount of moisture it can carry, is determined by its temperature. Warm moist air on the surface of the sea tends to rise, cooling as it does so, and condense out excess moisture in the form of cloud or rain (just as the warm air inside your car mists over the inside of a cold windscreen). Denser cold air, on the other hand, tends to sink. So the Atlantic's polar front, along which moving air masses of different temperatures tend to meet and swirl, is an area of complex instability.

The most prominent single feature of the weather along the coastlines of NW Europe is a **depression**. Somewhere out in the Atlantic, a bulge of warm subtropical air pushes into a cooler northern air mass and begins to swirl upwards. The bulge becomes a wave, with a **warm front** on its leading edge and a **cold front** trailing behind as cooler air closes in behind it. And if the cold front eventually overtakes the warm front, cutting off its supply of warm air, the fronts are said to be **occluded**.

The depression is therefore an area of ascending air and low pressure, and commonly referred to simply as a '**low**' – the term we shall mainly use from now on. A complete area of relatively high pressure, where cool air gently descends, is known as an **anticyclone** (the opposite word, cyclone, is reserved for vigorous tropical depressions) or just a '**high**'.

Pressure is measured in millibars with a **barometer** – a vital piece of marine equipment in the days before weather forecasts. The pressures that concern us fluctuate around the 1000 millibar level, with less than 940 millibars indicating a really deep low, and more than 1040 millibars an intense high, ie a range of about 100 millibars. Lows may be divided by a **ridge of high pressure**. Depressions have **troughs of low pressure**.

Meteorologists analyse such features by drawing maps, so-called **synoptic charts**, covered in **isobars** – ie lines of equal barometric pressure. These show the contours of a high or a low (just as height contours on a land map show the shape of the hills) which in turn indicate the strength and direction of the wind.

In the northern hemisphere **air circulates anti-clockwise round a low**, and slightly inwards towards the centre, while **round a high it circulates in the opposite direction, clockwise** and slightly outwards. Wind strength is determined by the pressure gradient – ie the steepness of the synoptic chart's contours – so **the closer the isobars, the stronger the winds.**

The shape of a low

Not all depressions come in from the Atlantic. But the classic pattern of British weather – and certainly the one most relevant to the Day Skipper course – is caused by a low tracking NE across the British Isles until it disappears somewhere over the Baltic. The clouds signalling its approach, the falling barometer, the wind shifts marking its contours – these are the raw material of those old weather sayings about mackerel skies and the moon hiding her head in a halo, explained later.

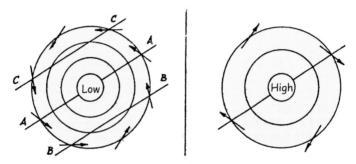

If you look at an isobaric diagram of a low, you will see that if it passes directly overhead, **the wind will shift**, after a brief lull sometimes referred to as 'the eye of the storm', through 180°, which is roughly from SE to NW (in our diagram, the observer's viewpoint moves along track A). If the centre of low pressure passes to the north (track B), a southerly wind will **veer** – that is, shift in a **clockwise direction** – until it becomes westerly. If the low passes to the south (track C), the wind will **back** – **anticlockwise** – from an easterly to a northerly direction. During the same period, the barometer will fall and rise.

A more realistic chart shows troughs of lower pressure accompanying the advancing warm and cold fronts, where the wind shifts will be sharper, especially at the passage of the cold front. And if this primary low has a secondary one developing on the tail of the cold front – perhaps eventually more violent than its parent – the wind may back sharply only to veer again.

But the first signs of an approaching low are likely to be visual – the wispy 'mares' tails' driven far ahead of it by strong, high altitude winds. Or as the old saying goes: *Mackerel sky and mares' tails, make tall ships carry small sails.*

Meteorologists distinguish **clouds** according to their height and form, and give them Latin names. For example the technical term for mares' tails is *cirrus* (from the Latin for a lock of hair). Fluffy white fine-weather clouds, like a child's picture book, are *cumulus* (from the Latin for heap). The term *stratus* (blanket) is used for layered cloud. So the combination *cirrostratus* describes the high-altitude layers which produce a 'halo' round the Sun or the Moon – another warning of bad weather because they stretch ahead of a depression. The Latin names don't necessarily matter, but as the old weather sayings suggest, the changing cloud formations themselves are fundamental indicators.

A large low pressure system may easily be 1000 miles in extent, with cloud stretching 500 miles ahead of the warm front. Its speed of movement can vary greatly – anything up to 60 knots – which is why the accurate timing of forecasts is so difficult. It can take all day for the first warning cloud signs to be translated into the rain and turbulence of the frontal areas.

Not that every depression produces rain. But assuming a vigorous low, with two distinct frontal troughs in the classic form, then the belt of rain along the warm front may be about 100 miles wide, and the cold front's rain belt perhaps 50 miles wide.

- **As the low approaches** the wind will back southerly and the sky begins to cloud over: high wispy streaks spreading to shroud the sun, then steadily lowering and darkening until rain begins to fall – light at first but soon settling into a continuous moderately heavy spell as the warm sector arrives.
- **Entering the warm sector,** fog or drizzle may reduce visibility even though the rain eases. The temperature will rise (though it may not *feel* warmer in these damp conditions).
- Yachtsmen will notice a veering wind, which should then stay steady until **the cold front arrives,** when it will veer again towards the north west, usually more sharply. The barometer will reflect the same pattern – steady, then rising rapidly. If the low is vigorous, with steep pressure gradients (closely spaced isobars) and correspondingly strong winds, this is when they will be felt.
- The **cold front** may bring heavy rain squalls. The gusty wind will accentuate cooler, fresher atmosphere. Towering thunder clouds may even produce some hail, but at least a cold front tends to pass more quickly than its warm counterpart. And above that brisk procession of heaped-up medium-level clouds, clear blue sky will soon be showing.

On land this is a cheerful moment – the arrival of 'showers and bright periods' after a spell of miserable wet weather. But at sea you can't relax yet. In fact you may need to pull down that last reef to weather the worst of the blow.

The high

At sea, just as on land, **high pressure generally means fine weather**. Pressure gradients round a high are usually less steep than in a low, so light winds are typical and gales rare. As the air descends, spreading outwards to feed neighbouring lows, it is compressed, warmed and dried. Moisture absorbed from the cold sea may condense out, but at this low level the incipient cloud is

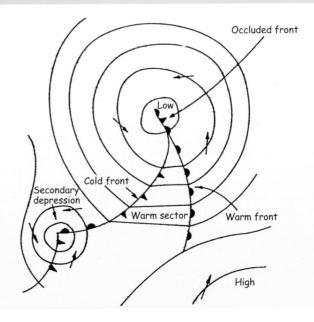

often stifled by a temperature inversion – a layer of warm air on top of the cooler surface air. So while anticyclonic weather may be dull and foggy, it seldom rains.

Local weather

For the short time most yachtsmen are at sea, local weather – such as sea breezes, violent squalls or fog – can be just as important as the big weather systems we have examined so far.

Coastal **sea breezes** are often produced in summer when rising air above the rapidly heated land surface sucks in air from offshore. At their peak on a hot afternoon, they may reach force 4–5, but not more, and die away at sunset. A sea breeze often gives yachtsmen a welcome lift home after a morning spent drifting; watch for a line of convective cumulus clouds building over the land, which may indicate that a breeze is developing.

At night, when the land cools more rapidly than the sea – whose temperature scarcely changes – the reverse process may produce a **land breeze**. This is usually a weak affair by comparison, but along a mountainous coastline, cold air rolling down the steep sides of a valley or fjord can produce a dangerous **katabatic wind**. Sudden, violent **squalls** can also be generated by the thermal up-draught at the base of a towering thunder cloud. It is often the lack of warning that makes a squall so alarming, not the actual weight of the wind. And the same applies to fog.

Current in restricted waters

Fog

Fog appears when air is cooled to the critical temperature (the dew point) below which it can no longer hold all its moisture as invisible vapour. Surplus moisture then condenses out as water droplets suspended in the air. The result is given various names, depending on the circumstances. **Frontal fog**, for example, occurs where warm and cold air mix. But the two main types are **radiation** or **land fog**, and **advection** or **sea fog**.

Land fog tends to occur, more often in autumn and winter, when any warmth in the land is rapidly radiated into a clear sky. It sometimes drifts out to sea for a few miles, particularly at dawn, when it is most prevalent.

Sea fog can arrive from land or sea. Air heated over continental Europe, for example, may release its moisture as it moves across the cool North Sea. Or fog can develop in the Channel, especially in spring and early summer, as a warm, moist, south westerly air stream from the Azores crosses progressively colder seas. It is the critical relationship of temperatures and humidity that matters, and once the potential for fog exists, a rising wind may not necessarily sweep it away. Sea fog can persist in force 5 or even 6. So it is vital to adopt the right tactics (discussed later) for dealing with it.

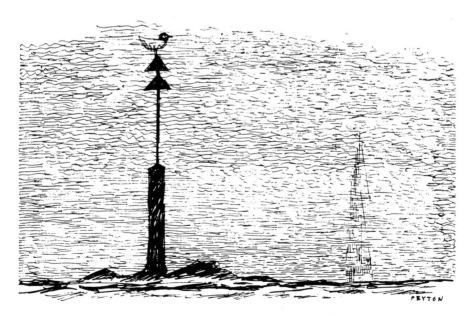

'What do you mean, "Beacon ahead." There's no beacon around here.'

'And stop saying "If I was at the navigation class I could ask Mr Hitchins".'

The Beaufort wind scale

This scale was devised in 1805 by Admiral Sir Francis Beaufort to relate various sea states to the amount of sail ships could carry – originally square-rigged naval frigates, later fishing smacks. Nowadays, it is widely used in weather forecasts, with appropriate descriptions of the effects on land and sea.

These can never be absolute. From the perspective of a small yacht, for example, there is an enormous difference between *running before* a given wind force and *beating back* into the same wind and sea. The waves don't change, but they feel quite different, especially when they are short and steep. On a coastal trip in heavy weather, the lie of the land also makes a critical difference, because waves cannot develop their full height unless they have a long uninterrupted 'fetch'. So a small boat can scuttle quickly along a sheltered coastline in conditions that might be unmanageable offshore.

With experience, yachtsmen relate the forecast wind force to the boats and sea areas they are familiar with – just as the Admiral did. Most people begin by exaggerating – force 6 is often tellingly referred to as 'a yachtsman's gale'. But then the written descriptions are not that much help. Nor is it easy to visualise conditions offshore when you are sitting in a sheltered harbour. But without some scale shipping forecasts would be much less concise and informative.

Ground track

Beaufort scale

Force	Wind speed in knots	Forecast description	Wave height in metres	Sea state	Effects on land
0	<1	Calm	0	Like a mirror	Smoke rises vertically
1	1–3	Light	0	Ripples without crests	Smoke, but not vanes, indicate wind direction
2	4–6	Light	0.1	Small wavelets, but crests do not break	Leaves rustle; wind vanes move
3	7–10	Light	0.4	Large wavelets; crests begin to break	Wind extends light flag
4	11–16	Moderate	1	Small waves; fairly frequent white horses	Wind raises dust and loose paper; small branches move
5	17–21	Fresh	2	Moderate, longer waves; many white horses	Small trees in leaf begin to sway
6	22–27	Strong breeze	3	Large waves with foam crests; spray likely	Telegraph wires whistle; umbrellas difficult to use
7	28–33	Near gale	4	Foam streaks begin to appear	Whole trees in motion
8	34–40	Gale	5.5	Longer waves, well marked with foam streaks	Twigs break off; walking is difficult
9	41–47	Severe gale	7	High waves with dense streaks of foam, spray and tumbling crests	Slight structural damage, eg to chimney pots and slates
10	48–55	Storm	9	Very high waves with long overhanging crests and large patches of foam; tumbling crests are heavy; visibility is affected	Trees uprooted; considerable structural damage

Weather information

Nearly all weather forecasts originate from the **Meteorological Office** at Exeter. The forecast office can be consulted directly – by telephone **(Metcall)**, fax **(Metfax)**, or internet: www.metoffice.gov.uk. But most yachtsmen use a variety of indirect sources: **BBC shipping forecasts**, **local radio broadcasts**, the **Marinecall** telephone service, **Navtex** (for which a special receiver is needed), **Coastguard** inshore forecasts, **television** and **newspapers**.

All of these are helpful in different ways. Television forecasts, for example, are an excellent way to get a general picture of the weather before setting sail, with bulletins often looking several days ahead. The BBC's presentation is especially thorough, using the professional terminology. Some newspapers also publish proper weather maps which can be taken aboard, although of course they are inevitably based on yesterday's information. The Coastguard's four-hourly inshore waters forecasts on VHF radio are particularly convenient for yachtsmen.

Pre-eminent among all these services is the BBC shipping forecast, with its concise, coded language and unchanging sequence. There is no RYA requirement to draw your own weather map, but if you want to have a go, this is your source. Using one of the RYA/R Met Soc '*Metmaps*' will make it a lot easier.

The shipping forecast

The Met Office prepares the shipping forecast four times a day for broadcast by BBC Radio 4 – currently issued at 0048, 0535, 1201 and 1754. The first two of these broadcasts are followed by a supplementary forecast for the inshore waters of the UK, divided into nine areas.

The main shipping forecast consists of four elements:

- Gale warnings – a summary of any warnings in force
- A general synopsis
- Area forecasts
- Reports from coastal stations (0048 and 0535 only)

The **synopsis** gives the position of the main lows, highs, troughs and fronts from the latest analysis by the central forecast office (that is about 6 hours previously), the central pressure of lows and highs, and their expected movement over the next 24 hours.

Sea **area forecasts** come next, always in the same order, starting with Viking, off Norway, then clockwise round the British Isles through Humber and Thames, Wight and Portland, Rockall and Malin, to finish in South East Iceland. For each area, details are given of changing wind, weather and visibility for the next 24 hours.

Estimated position

'Did you catch the forecast?'

The 5-minute bulletin ends twice a day with **reports from coastal stations** in a similar clockwise sequence – currently Tiree, Stornaway, Lerwick, Fife Ness, Bridlington, Sandettie light vessel, Greenwich light vessel, Jersey, Channel light vessel, Scilly, Valentia, Ronaldsway and Malin Head – describing the local wind direction and force, the weather, the visibility in miles or metres, the atmospheric pressure in millibars and how it is changing.

The language of these forecasts is precise and economical. Their ritual pattern fascinates even landlubbers with not the slightest interest in whether it is blowing an easterly gale off the Humber. Superfluous words like 'wind force' and 'visibility' are omitted, while those included each have a careful definition. Giving the forecast for sea area Portland, for example, the BBC announcer might simply say: 'NORTHWESTERLY 6, FAIR, GOOD', meaning that the wind will blow from the NW at force 6 (22–27 knots), the weather will be fair (ie no rain showers, mist or fog) and the visibility good (more than 5 miles).

The definitions may seem arbitrary, but they should be learned, both to understand the forecast and because they may be the subject of specific questions in an assessment paper.

Terminology in shipping forecasts

Wind speeds – measured on Beaufort Scale

Wind shifts
- **Veering** – clockwise shift eg from NE to SE
- **Backing** – anticlockwise shift eg from NW to SW

Gale warnings
- **Gales** – mean wind speeds of F8 (34–40 knots) or gusts of more than 43 knots
- **Severe gales** – mean wind speed of F9 (41–47 knots) or gusts of more than 51 knots

Timing
- **Imminent** – within 6 hours
- **Soon** – in 6 to 12 hours
- **Later** – in more than 12 hours

Visibility
- **Good** – more than 5 nautical miles
- **Moderate** – 2 to 5 nautical miles
- **Poor** – 1000 metres to 2 nautical miles
- **Fog** – less than 1000 metres

Weather
- **Fair** – no rain, mist or fog

Points to remember about weather

- Winds blow anticlockwise round a *low*, clockwise round a *high*.
- Fronts produce wind shifts.
- On a synoptic chart, the closer the isobars, the stronger the winds.
- Warm front (of a low) – wet, windy, poor visibility.
- Cold front (of a low) – squalls, showers, good visibility.
- High – moderate winds, good weather but sometimes poor visibility.
- Local weather may be more important than general situation.
- Sea fog can persist even in a fresh wind.
- Bad timing may turn a correct forecast into a crucially wrong one.

Flashing light (Fl) – dark period exceeds light

To take all this information down at the speed a BBC announcer reads, you need a few shorthand symbols, however informal. L and H are obvious for low and high; wind directions and forces record naturally as letters and numbers; a horizontal arrow can show that something – perhaps a wind direction – is 'becoming' something else; an oblique line will indicate the forecaster's habitual distinction between the situation 'at first' and 'later'. But unless you are attempting your own weather map, you will usually need only the general synopsis and your local area forecast.

Coping with bad weather

When people talk about bad weather at sea, they normally mean a gale. But there are situations when fog can be more dangerous – for example a crowded shipping lane like the Dover Strait, half choked with sandbanks and a ship thudding past every five minutes.

Sea fog, as we have seen, can be accompanied by a fresh breeze, but then again the yacht may be virtually becalmed, and dependent on her auxiliary engine to take avoiding action. Motoring in these conditions is problematic – it is harder to hear danger approaching, but easier to get out of the way if it suddenly appears out of the murk. Stopping the engine periodically to listen is probably the best tactic. Whatever else, your engine should be warmed up and ready for instant use.

At the first suspicion of advancing fog, it is vital to plot an accurate position. Other commonsense precautions include wearing lifejackets, having a dinghy towing or ready to launch, and using a foghorn. (It will not be heard on a ship's bridge in time to make any difference, but other yachts will be alerted.) In many situations the safest course is to sound your way into shallow water where large vessels cannot follow, or at least keep clear of the shipping lanes.

Fog precautions

- Plot position at first sign of worsening visibility.
- Maintain plot eg with GPS.
- Hoist radar reflector if not permanently rigged.
- Put on lifejackets.
- Launch or at least prepare dinghy.
- Increase lookout and, if under power, stop engine periodically to listen.
- Sound foghorn every two minutes.
- Consider sounding into shallow water.

Since almost everything aboard a small boat in **rough weather** is more difficult – even just moving about, or boiling a kettle – the key to surviving it in relative comfort and safety is anticipation. This starts with the weather forecast and culminates in a strategic choice – whether to run for shelter or find some sea room to ride it out.

The aim is to minimise what has to be done during a blow by thinking ahead – putting on oilskins before you get wet, closing hatches, stowing loose gear securely, getting out safety harnesses, shortening sail early (before you really need to, unless of course you are racing), preparing some simple food, looking up navigational data you may need, planning an escape route if gear failure forces you to run off downwind, and so on. And if you suffer from seasickness, take the tablets early.

When heavy weather cannot be avoided, the way to make it relatively comfortable is to pull down one more reef than you absolutely need. And if there's a job to do on deck, don't forget the ancient tactic of 'heaving-to' (jib aback, mainsail close hauled and helm lashed down); it really transforms the situation.

Heavy weather checklist

- Secure loose gear on deck and below.
- Put on lifejackets and safety harnesses.
- Take seasickness tablets if required.
- Take in reef or reefs (maybe one more than immediately required).
- Rig jackstays if not permanent.
- Prepare simple food in accessible locker.
- Pre-plan navigation and escape routes.

'Its definitely thickening.'

Warm front

Anchoring

A cruising yacht should carry two anchors: a main **bower** and a smaller **kedge**, which is easier to handle and lay out from a dinghy.

There are five main anchor designs, each with their pros and cons:

- **Fisherman** – the oldest form, dismantles to stow flat, provides relatively poor holding except in weed or rocks, when it may hold better than the others.
- **Danforth** – its main advantage is the flat stowage.
- **Plough or CQR** – relatively good holding for a given weight, especially in mud or sand, but awkward to stow.
- **Delta** – a plough variant designed for self-launching and retrieval.
- **Bruce** – developed for oil rigs, good holding in soft ground, awkward to stow but no moving parts to crush fingers.

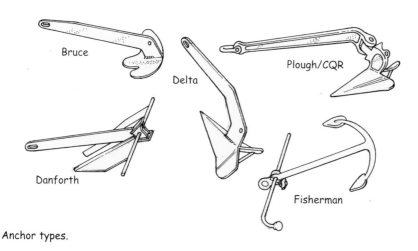

Bruce

Delta

Plough/CQR

Danforth

Fisherman

Anchor types.

When **choosing an anchorage**, the first things to establish are:

- The **depth of water** at low tide.
- The **nature of the seabed** – Mud? Sand? Rocks? Flat or steeply shelving?

As a rough rule, if your anchor is attached to **chain, let out at least four times the depth**. The weight of the chain helps stabilise the boat and ensures that the pull on the anchor is horizontal, to dig it in. Flake some chain out on deck before you let go, and it helps to have a few depths marked on the chain eg with paint.

With **warp** (preferably plaited nylon) use **at least six times the depth**, but you should in any case have a few metres of chain next to the anchor, to provide some weight and prevent chafe. If in doubt, let out a bit more, and if you are still worried, don't hesitate to up anchor and try again.

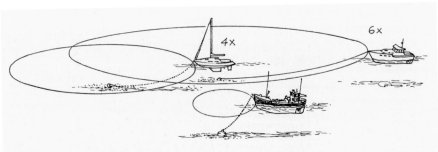

An anchorage showing the 'sailing circles' of: a yacht on 4x chain, a motor cruiser on 6x warp and a fishing boat on a fixed mooring.

Boats anchored with warp tend to 'sail' around, so beware of that when you choose your own spot. Those on shorter fixed moorings will move less, but watch that the mooring's ground chain does not foul your anchor. A buoyed 'tripping' line is one answer, to yank the anchor out the way it went in, although it is often more trouble than it is worth.

Before finally dropping the hook, visualise the anchorage when the tide turns and in the worst conditions you are likely to encounter before you leave. Would you have room to sail the anchor out at low water in a freshening onshore wind?

Direction of buoyage

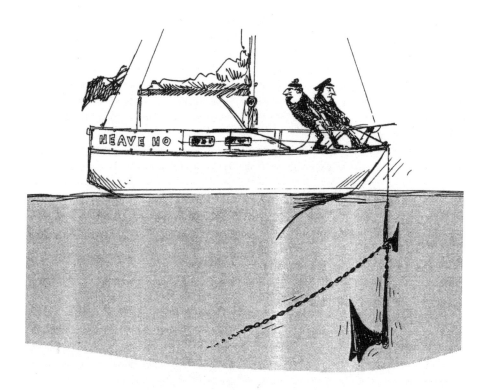

'We're not the only ones with problems. That big ketch behind is dragging, and fast.'

Passage planning

The Maritime and Coastguard Agency (MCA) now require all skippers to prepare a passage plan before going to sea. How detailed this is depends on the size of boat, number of crew and extent of voyage. For guidelines see the box on page 53.

Anything that can be done in advance, before leaving harbour, will probably be easier than at sea – sorting out charts, programming the GPS, looking up harbour entrance signals, noting the times of high water, plotting a couple of likely courses, and so on.

Also, a lot of time can be saved, by working your tides along a coastline instead of battling against them. Heading for a river entrance with a difficult bar, or a shallow swatchway through the sands, you can avoid a lot of anxiety by arriving on the flood.

Take, as an example, a coastal passage in an 8-metre sloop from Burnham-on-Crouch, in Essex, to Felixstowe Ferry, at the entrance to the River Deben in Suffolk – about 35–40 nautical miles, depending on the exact track. This is how we might think it through the night before setting sail:

'I know we didn't do it like this at Nav classes . . .'

Position of fog signal

- To plan our passage, we need a **small scale chart**. Our sketch chart (on the next page) shows the main features of the trip, starting from a mooring off Burnham – down the estuary of the River Crouch, through the coastal sandbanks, across the approaches to the big commercial port of Harwich, and finally over the half-tide bar of the River Deben into what is known as Woodbridge Haven.
- The almanac's **tide tables** predict HW at Burnham-on-Crouch at 06.45 UT (07.45 BST), which in this part of the world means a neap tide – neither very high nor very low, with gentle tidal streams.
- The **weather forecast** suggests a light southerly wind becoming moderate south easterly as a sea breeze sets in during the afternoon. So, a quiet misty start and a brisk sail later in the day – benign conditions in which to try out our Day Skipper skills.
- A glance at the **tidal atlas** (or **tidal diamonds M, K** and **F**) shows the tide flooding in a south-westerly direction, roughly parallel with the coast, and ebbing to the north east. Neaps run at no more than about 1½ knots – an average of, say, 1 knot. In light to moderate winds our boat should average perhaps 4 knots through the water. So if we time our departure to make full use of the tide, the trip will take about 7–8 hours; or if much of it is spent struggling against the tide, perhaps 10–11 hours.
- The crux of the trip is evidently crossing the shallow, sandy bar which blocks the mouth of the Deben. For this we have obtained a **large scale sketch chart**, prepared by the Felixstowe Ferry harbourmaster, and frequently updated

---

MCA guidelines for passage planning

- **Weather** Get a reliable weather forecast before departing.
- **Tides** Use tide tables to check the tides in the area where you are cruising.
- **Limitations of the vessel** Is your boat fit for the voyage? Do you have adequate safety equipment, including a suitable radio?
- **Crew** Assess the capabilities of your crew members. Will they be able to cope on the voyage?
- **Navigational hazards** Do you know what hazards you are likely to face on passage? Have you plotted your route properly with a chart and pilot book?
- **Back-up plan** You will need a back-up plan in case the weather deteriorates or some other unforeseen problem crops up. Can you navigate without your GPS set?
- **On shore** Make sure that someone ashore knows your plan, details of your boat and has the correct contact number for the Coast-guard in the event that you are overdue and there is concern for your safety.

⚓ Sp

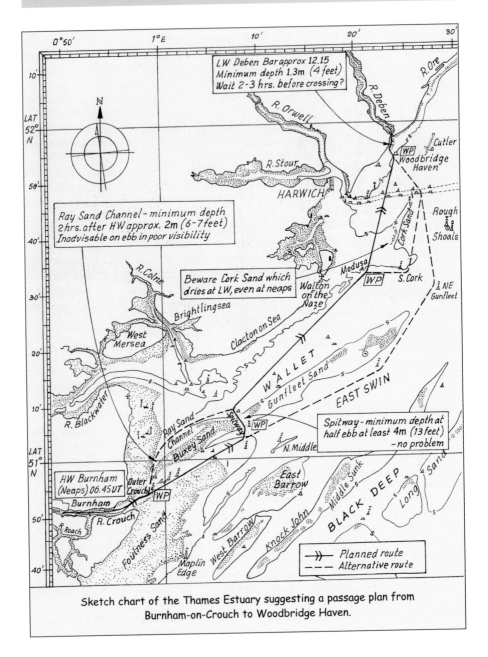

Sketch chart of the Thames Estuary suggesting a passage plan from Burnham-on-Crouch to Woodbridge Haven.

Church spire

'Purely as a matter of interest, Joe, would you glance at the chart and tell me if the soundings are marked in fathoms or metres?'

because the sands are always shifting. It shows a minimum depth just inside the buoyed entrance channel of 0.8m (about 2½ feet) at LW Springs. But on a neap tide like tomorrow's, according to the local pilot book, there will be about 0.5m more than this at LW ie a minimum of 1.3m. If these figures were absolutely precise (which they cannot be), and it was flat calm, there would be just enough water for our boat's draught of 1.2m (4 feet) – but no margin for error. So how long should we wait before entering? A couple of hours?

- Consulting the **almanac**, the tide tables for nearby Walton-on-Naze show a range of only 1.9m (6 feet) – an exceptionally weak tide. When this range is applied to the tidal curve, it shows a rise of just 0.5m in the first two hours (about 1½ feet), closely matching the Rule of Twelfths (³/₁₂ths of 6 feet). That should be enough – unless the onshore breeze freshens more than expected. To be completely sure, we can aim for 3 hours after LW, when a rise of 1.0m gives plenty of water under the keel.
- So what time is LW at the Deben bar? The **local pilot book** suggests 45 minutes earlier than at Burnham ie about 12.15. So we want to reach the entrance some time after 15.15, but not much later than 18.30, when the ebb begins to flow

G

out of the river. Working back from this, we should drop the Burnham mooring at, or shortly after, HW, allowing up to about 11 hours for the passage.
- On leaving the River Crouch, there is a basic choice: to take the rather longer track outside the Buxey, Gunfleet and Cork sands, or cut inside through one of the swatchways – which is what we decide to do.
- Soon after clearing the land, we could slide northwards through the Ray Sand Channel. The shallowest section of this route evidently dries 1.4m (4½ feet) at very low tides (ie at chart datum), so even tomorrow it will be dry at LW. On the other hand the tidal range in the Crouch is a bit larger at 2.8m (9 feet), so by the time we reach the channel, there should still be 6–7 feet of water. Fine in theory, but there will probably be some mist about, and this is not a good place to run aground on an ebbing tide. Better follow the main channel out to the end of the Whitaker Spit and turn N through the Spitway, where the chart shows a minimum depth of 1.6m. At half-ebb there will be plenty of water – more than 4.0m (13 feet).
- The narrow entrance to the Crouch is well buoyed, but with poor visibility in prospect, it is worth pre-programming a couple of **GPS waypoints** – at the Buxey Sand bottleneck and the southern end of the Spitway. But when using GPS, remember to back it up by logging other navigational information.
- Once in the Wallet, we can if need be track another waypoint near the Medusa buoy, marking the southern approaches to Harwich harbour. But there are plenty of good **visual references**, such as the 80-foot Naze Tower. By the time we're off there it will be LW, so even at neaps we shall need to go firmly inside or outside the Cork Sand, which dries more than a metre at chart datum (a GPS **clearing line** might be useful, depending on the visibility) before picking our moment to cross the busy Harwich approach channel – if necessary with a burst of engine – and laying a course for the Woodbridge Haven buoy.
- If we miss the tide altogether, or there is some other problem, the wide deep-water entrance to Harwich is conveniently downwind, with a choice of anchorages and marinas. There is a 'recommended yacht track' S and W of the dredged channel, so we should not need to tangle with the big ships coming and going.

Points to remember about making a passage plan

- Select small scale chart – choose best route to avoid hazards, optimise tides and landfalls.
- Add large scale charts, harbour plans and pilot book – for destination and possible diversions.
- Note times of HW and LW; check tidal streams.
- Note relevant GPS waypoints, lights, harbour signals, limiting depths, clearing lines.
- Check fuel against requirements.
- Obtain weather forecast.
- Plot initial track.

Starboard hand buoy

The rule of the road

Even the most inveterate landlubber probably knows that ships carry a green navigation light on their starboard side and a red one to port, or that steam traditionally gives way to sail. Such basic principles evolved over centuries as part of what maritime lawyers call 'the ordinary practice of seamen'.

Nowadays they are codified, along with many much more complex rules, in the *International Regulations for Preventing Collisions at Sea* – the **colregs** for short. The current regulations date from 1972, since when they have several times been amended. The fundamental principle of steam giving way to sail has survived, but only just. It is severely limited by other rules giving priority to large commercial craft.

The regulations come in **four parts**:

A – general rules and definitions
B – steering and sailing rules
C – lights and shapes
D – sound and light signals

These rules form an important part of the Day Skipper course because they are mostly of immediate practical importance, whether you command a 5-ton yacht or a 50,000-ton tanker. Going to sea with no knowledge of the steering rules would be like driving a car without knowing which way to go round a roundabout.

Our book therefore presents the steering and sailing rules virtually complete (because here the RYA expects you to acquire a 'full' knowledge), and summarises the other three sections (where only a 'working' knowledge is required). But to make this large chunk of text digestible, we have added explanatory notes and used a variety of typefaces for different sorts of information.

The TEXT IN CAPITALS indicates KEY PHRASES, or in some cases complete rules, that may be worth skimming through just before the examination. Less important sections of the rules are [paraphrased in square brackets]. *Text in italic* denotes rules that are of *direct or special relevance to yachtsmen*. Explanatory notes and comments are tinted.

International Regulations for Preventing Collisions at Sea, 1972

PART A – General Rules and Definitions

A mass of legal language in which a few items of immediate practical importance are buried.

Rule 1 – Application

a) These RULES shall APPLY TO ALL VESSELS UPON THE HIGH SEAS and in all waters connected therewith navigable by seagoing vessels [but governments can make special rules for warships and fishing vessels].

Rule 2 – Responsibility

A reminder that pedantic compliance with the written rules is not enough, either at sea or in court, because they may be overridden by special circumstances, or the 'ordinary practice of seamen'.

Rule 3 – General definitions

Worth glancing through because one or two of them – such as Rule 3c – may surprise you.

For the purpose of these rules, except where the context otherwise requires:

a) The word 'VESSEL' includes EVERY DESCRIPTION OF WATER CRAFT, including non-displacement craft and seaplanes...

b) The term 'POWER-DRIVEN VESSEL' means any vessel PROPELLED BY MACHINERY.

c) *The term 'SAILING VESSEL' means any vessel UNDER SAIL PROVIDED THAT PROPELLING MACHINERY, IF FITTED, IS NOT BEING USED.*

A sailing yacht with her auxiliary engine running is treated as a power-boat.

d) The term 'VESSEL ENGAGED IN FISHING' means any vessel fishing with nets, lines, trawls or other fishing apparatus which restrict manoeuvrability...

e) [definition of a seaplane]

f) The term 'VESSEL NOT UNDER COMMAND' means a vessel which THROUGH SOME EXCEPTIONAL CIRCUMSTANCES is UNABLE TO MANOEUVRE AS REQUIRED BY THESE RULES and is therefore unable to keep out of the way of another vessel.

'Before you turn in, left is port is red. Correct?'

g) The term ' RESTRICTED IN HER ABILITY TO MANOEUVRE' means a vessel which FROM THE NATURE OF HER WORK IS RESTRICTED in her ability to manoeuvre... [examples include cable layers, dredgers, buoy tenders, survey ships, tugs engaged in towing, and warships minesweeping or launching aircraft]

h) The term 'VESSEL CONSTRAINED BY HER DRAUGHT' means a power-driven vessel which, because of her draught in relation to the available depth and width of navigable water, is SEVERELY RESTRICTED IN HER ABILITY TO DEVIATE from the course she is following.

i) The term 'UNDER WAY' means that a vessel is NOT AT ANCHOR, OR MADE FAST TO THE SHORE, OR AGROUND.

Note that being 'under way' is not the same as 'making way through the water'.

j) [definitions of dimensions]

k) Vessels shall be deemed to be IN SIGHT of one another ONLY WHEN ONE CAN BE OBSERVED VISUALLY FROM THE OTHER.

A radar echo does not count as 'seeing'.

PART B – Steering and Sailing Rules

Section 1 – Conduct of vessels in any condition of visibility

> More definitions, and some good practical advice, such as making bold, early changes of course when avoiding collision, so the other vessel can clearly see your intention; and notice Rule 10 about crossing traffic separation schemes, to avoid 'impeding the passage' of large commercial craft.

Rule 4 – [rules apply in any visibility]

Rule 5 – Look-out

Every vessel shall AT ALL TIMES MAINTAIN A PROPER LOOK-OUT by sight and hearing as well as BY ALL AVAILABLE MEANS appropriate in the prevailing circumstances and conditions so as to make a full appraisal of the situation and the risk of collision.

> No guarantee that a large ship will notice a small yacht under her bows.

Rule 6 – Safe speed

Every vessel shall at all times proceed at a safe speed so that she can take proper and effective action to avoid collision and be stopped within a distance appropriate to the prevailing circumstances and conditions.

Rule 7 – Risk of collision

a) Every vessel shall use all available means appropriate to the prevailing circumstances and conditions to determine if risk of collision exists. If there is any doubt, such risk shall be deemed to exist.

b) Proper use shall be made of radar equipment if fitted and operational, including long-range scanning to obtain early warning of risk of collision and radar plotting or equivalent systematic observation of detected objects.

> In order to avoid the notorious 'radar-assisted' collision.

c) Assumptions shall not be made on the basis of scanty information, especially scanty radar information.

d) In determining if risk of collision exists, the following considerations shall be among those taken into account:

    (i)   SUCH RISK shall be deemed to exist IF THE COMPASS BEARING OF AN APPROACHING VESSEL DOES NOT APPRECIABLY CHANGE.

> This is not just a legal definition – it is the best way of telling that a collision risk exists.

Transferred position line

CARDINAL MARKS

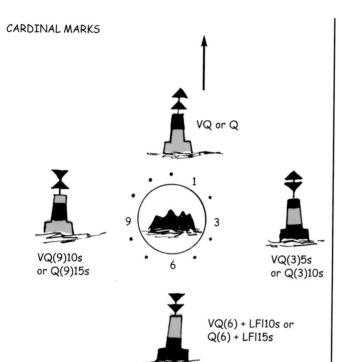

Special mark –
shape optional –
has a yellow light
(any rhythm)

VQ or Q

VQ(9)10s
or Q(9)15s

VQ(3)5s
or Q(3)10s

VQ(6) + LFl10s or
Q(6) + LFl15s

The characteristics of cardinal buoys are easily remembered. The top marks point up (North), down (South), together (West, like a wineglass), and the one with bases together must be East (like an egg). The black sections of the buoy are also where the top marks point. The characteristics of the lights are as on a clock face: three, six and nine. The odd one out – instead of twelve, one.

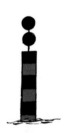

Isolated danger mark could be a buoy of any shape; light white Gp Fl (2) – remember 2 spheres and Gp Fl (2)

LATERAL MARKS

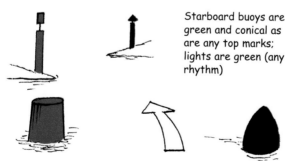

Starboard buoys are green and conical as are any top marks; lights are green (any rhythm)

Safe water mark can also be a spherical buoy or beacon; light is white isophase, occulting or one long flash every 10 seconds

Lateral buoys are usually related to the flood tide with; port hand buoys are red and flat topped, as are any top marks; lights are red (any rhythm).

ENGLAND – SOUTH COAST

DOVER STRAIT

North Foreland to
Beachy Head and Boulogne

SOUNDINGS in METRES

Depths are reduced to Chart Datum, which is approximately the level of Lowest Astronomical Tide (L.A.T.)

Positions are referred to Ordnance Survey of Great Britain (1936) Datum

Underlined figures on drying banks denote heights in metres and decimetres above Low Water

Other heights shown are in metres above High Water

Areas drying at Low Water coloured Yellow

Depths of between 0 and 5 metres shown White

Depths of over 5 metres coloured Blue

Natural Scale at Lat. 51° 00' N. – 1:113 000

Projection – Mercator

Extract from Imray Chart No C8 Dover Strait

Approximate Direction & Rate of Tidal Streams
Based upon H.W. at DOVER

Position 51°09'·0N 1°27'·8E ⓖ		Hours before H.W.						HW	Hours after H.W					
		6	5	4	3	2	1	HW	1	2	3	4	5	6
Direction		212	213	216	228		032	Slack	038	039	034	031	Slack	203	210
Rate in Knots	Springs	2·2	2·2	1·9	1·3		1·2		2·0	2·3	2·2	1·5		1·0	1·8
	Neaps	1·2	1·2	1·1	0·8		0·7		1·2	1·3	1·2	0·8		0·6	1·0

Sandwic

Depths, contours and colour codes The figures on the chart indicate depths in metres. If you look at the inner contour line on the blue area, you will see that it indicates a safe (for yachts) 5 metre depth. White areas indicate shallows between 0 and 5 metres while yellow patches show areas drying at low water (LW), such as the Goodwin Sands. Elsewhere contours show deeper channels and scattered numbers give spot depths.

Symbols There are many symbols and abbreviations; examples are the three types of wreck symbol: a drawing of a sinking ship indicates a wreck showing any part at the level of chart datum; Wk next to a circled figure shows the depth obtained by sounding; a horizontal line with three graded vertical line a wreck at unknown depth which is not considered dangerous.

Lights and buoys At the top of the chart the N Foreland lighthouse marks the headland with 5 flashes every 20 seconds with a red northerly sector to warn vessels clear. Red (port) and green (starboard) buoys delineate channels as with the southern approach to Ramsgate. Cardinal buoys such as the NW Goodwin bell buoy mark danger.

Shipping lanes The purple line near the compass rose (bottom right corner) marks the edge of the traffic separation zone.

Tidal streams The circled letter G near the SW Goodwin buoy (on Admiralty charts these are a diamond shape) refers to the table of tidal streams before and after HW Dover, printed over the green land area. The same information can also be obtained from chartlets (top left) where the double set of figures refer to the tidal speeds in knots at neaps and springs.

Landmarks Conspicuous landmarks like the cooling towers over Pegwell bay are often visible when inshore buoys are still well below the horizon. Look for symbols for castles, churches, water towers and radio masts.

DGPS has been developed to give a greater accuracy than the Precise Positioning Service. In order to make use of DGPS corrections, which are transmitted in a coded

Dover

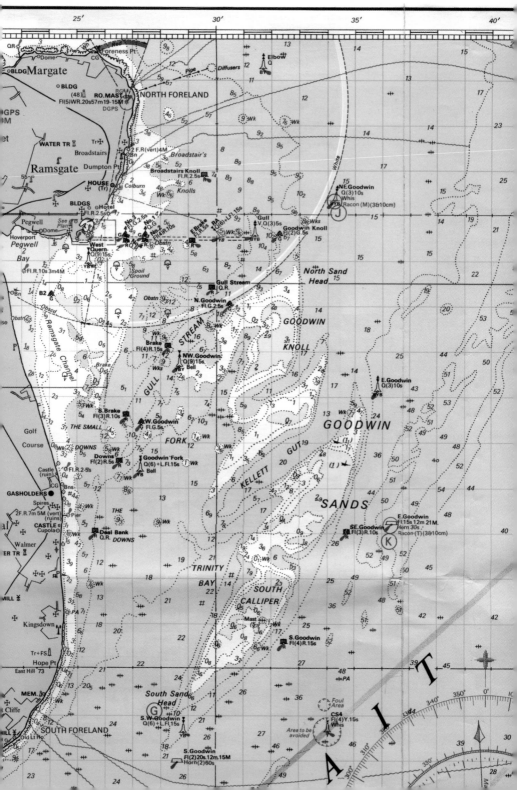

POWER DRIVEN VESSELS UNDER WAY

bow view of vessel less than 50m

port

stern

bow view of vessel more than 50m

port

the number of masthead lights - two compulsory over 50m but only one compulsory under 50m - indicate the vessel's length whatever her type

stern

flashing

air cushion vessel – bow view

flashing

port less than 50m

flashing

stern

vessel under 7m - white all-round light

TOWING AND PUSHING

bow

tug less than 50m with length of tow more than 200m

bow tug more than 50m

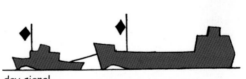

day signal

stern view, any length

tug more than 50m with length of tow more than 200m

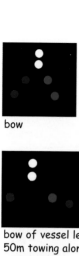

bow

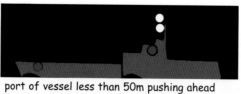

port of vessel less than 50m pushing ahead

stern

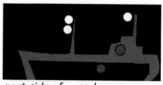

bow of vessel less than
50m towing alongside

port side of vessel more
than 50m

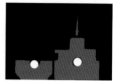

stern

bow

port

stern

sailing vessel making way

FISHING VESSELS

bow of trawler
not making way

port side of trawler more than 50m
making way

day signal

not making way

surface net fishing vessel
making way - port side

stern making way

bow not
making way

making way - port side, nets
extending more than 150m
from vessel

stern making way
(additional light
shows direction
of gear)

day signal

VESSELS NOT UNDER COMMAND OR RESTRICTED IN THEIR ABILITY TO MANOEUVRE

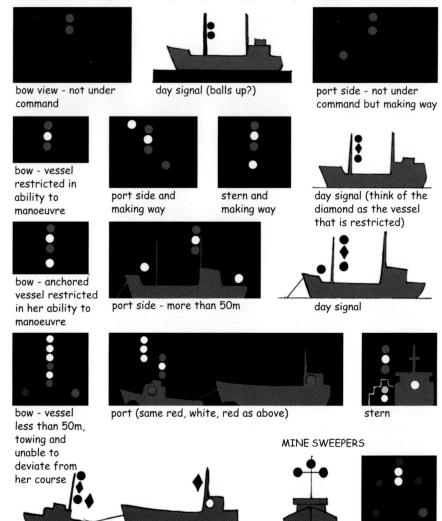

bow view - not under command

day signal (balls up?)

port side - not under command but making way

bow - vessel restricted in ability to manoeuvre

port side and making way

stern and making way

day signal (think of the diamond as the vessel that is restricted)

bow - anchored vessel restricted in her ability to manoeuvre

port side - more than 50m

day signal

bow - vessel less than 50m, towing and unable to deviate from her course

port (same red, white, red as above)

stern

MINE SWEEPERS

day signals

day signal

bow making way

DREDGERS

bow not making way (double red lights indicate obstructed side)

day signal

When the size of the vessel prevents these shapes being shown, a vessel engaged in under-water operations should fly the code flag A

VESSELS CONSTRAINED BY THEIR DRAUGHT

bow

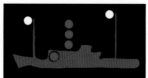

more than 50m – port side

stern

day signal

PILOT VESSELS

bow - at anchor

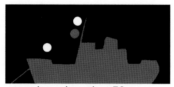

at anchor - less than 50m - port side

stern - making way

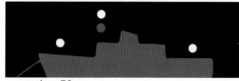

more than 50m

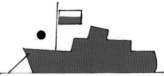

day signal - the red and white of the all-round lights are duplicated in the day signal

ANCHORED VESSELS AND VESSELS AGROUND

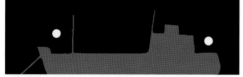

at anchor - more than 50m - port side

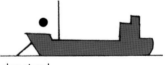

day signal

bow

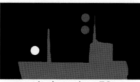

aground - less than 50m

stern

day signal

aground – more than 50m (note preponderance of port red lights)

SEAPLANES

bow

port side   stern

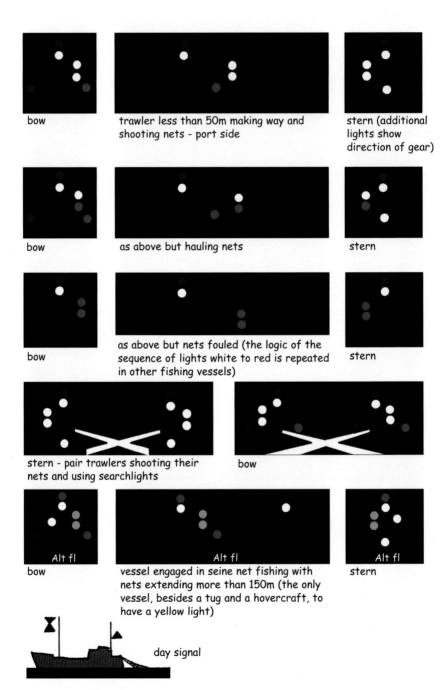

bow

trawler less than 50m making way and shooting nets - port side

stern (additional lights show direction of gear)

bow

as above but hauling nets

stern

bow

as above but nets fouled (the logic of the sequence of lights white to red is repeated in other fishing vessels)

stern

stern - pair trawlers shooting their nets and using searchlights

bow

Alt fl

bow

Alt fl

vessel engaged in seine net fishing with nets extending more than 150m (the only vessel, besides a tug and a hovercraft, to have a yellow light)

Alt fl

stern

day signal

(ii)   Such risk may sometimes exist even when an appreciable bearing change is evident, particularly when approaching a very large vessel, or a tow, or when approaching a vessel at close range.

Rule 8 – Action to avoid collision

a) Any ACTION TO AVOID COLLISION shall, if the circumstances of the case admit, be POSITIVE, made IN AMPLE TIME and with due regard to the observance of good seamanship.

b) ANY ALTERATION OF COURSE AND/OR SPEED to avoid collision shall, if the circumstances of the case permit, be LARGE ENOUGH TO BE READILY APPARENT TO ANOTHER VESSEL OBSERVING VISUALLY OR BY RADAR; a succession of small alterations of course and/or speed should be avoided.

Excellent practical advice, especially when manoeuvring to avoid large cumbersome ships.

c) If there is sufficient sea room, alteration of course alone may be the most effective action to avoid a close-quarters situation...

d) [pass at a 'safe' distance]

e) [if necessary, slacken speed or even stop]

f) [this rule does not contradict rules about 'not impeding passage']

Rule 9 – Narrow channels

a) A VESSEL proceeding along the course of a narrow channel or fairway SHALL KEEP as near TO THE OUTER LIMIT OF THE CHANNEL OR FAIRWAY WHICH LIES ON HER STARBOARD SIDE as is safe and practicable.

b) *A vessel of less than 20 metres in length or a SAILING VESSEL SHALL NOT IMPEDE THE PASSAGE OF A VESSEL WHICH CAN SAFELY NAVIGATE ONLY WITHIN A NARROW CHANNEL or fairway.*

c) A VESSEL ENGAGED IN FISHING SHALL NOT IMPEDE THE PASSAGE of any other vessel navigating within a narrow channel or fairway.

d) A VESSEL SHALL NOT CROSS A NARROW CHANNEL OR FAIRWAY IF SUCH CROSSING IMPEDES the passage of a vessel which can safely navigate only within such channel or fairway. The latter vessel may use the sound signal prescribed in Rule 34d

(Five short and rapid blasts.)

if in doubt as to the intention of the crossing vessel.

e) (i)   In a narrow channel or fairway when overtaking can take place only if the vessel to be overtaken takes action to permit safe passing, the VESSEL INTENDING TO OVERTAKE shall indicate her intention by SOUNDING THE APPROPRIATE SIGNAL prescribed in Rule 34c (i).

(Two long and one short blasts if overtaking to starboard; two long and two short to port.)

The VESSEL TO BE OVERTAKEN shall, IF IN AGREEMENT, SOUND THE APPROPRIATE SIGNAL prescribed in Rule 34c (ii)

(Long, short, long, short blasts.)

and take steps to permit safe passing. IF IN DOUBT she MAY SOUND THE SIGNALS prescribed in Rule 34d

(Five short and rapid blasts.)

   (ii)   [Rule 13 still applies ie keep clear when overtaking]

f) A VESSEL NEARING A BEND or an area of a narrow channel or fairway where other vessels may be obscured by an intervening obstruction shall navigate with particular alertness and caution and shall SOUND THE APPROPRIATE SIGNAL prescribed in Rule 34e

(One long blast.)

g) [if possible avoid anchoring in a narrow channel]

Rule 10 – Traffic Separation Schemes

a) This rule applies to traffic separation schemes adopted by IMO (International Maritime Organisation) and does not relieve any vessel of her obligation under any other rule.

b) A VESSEL USING A TRAFFIC SCHEME shall:

   (i)   PROCEED in the appropriate traffic lane IN THE GENERAL DIRECTION OF TRAFFIC for that lane;

   (ii) So far as practicable KEEP CLEAR OF A TRAFFIC SEPARATION LINE OR SEPARATION ZONE;

   (iii) NORMALLY JOIN OR LEAVE A TRAFFIC LANE AT THE TERMINATION of the lane...

c) A VESSEL SHALL so far as practicable avoid crossing traffic lanes, but if obliged to do so, shall CROSS ON A HEADING AS NEARLY AS PRACTICABLE AT RIGHT ANGLES TO THE GENERAL DIRECTION OF TRAFFIC FLOW.

Particularly important for yachts crossing the crowded Dover Strait. The aim is to minimise the time spent in traffic lanes by steering straight across instead of heading up-tide to make good a right-angled course.

d) Inshore traffic zones shall not normally be used by through traffic which can safely use the appropriate traffic lane within the adjacent traffic separation scheme. However *VESSELS OF LESS THAN 20 METRES IN LENGTH AND SAILING VESSELS MAY UNDER ALL CIRCUMSTANCES USE INSHORE TRAFFIC ZONES.*

e) A VESSEL OTHER THAN A CROSSING VESSEL or a vessel joining or leaving a lane shall NOT NORMALLY ENTER A SEPARATION ZONE or cross a separation line EXCEPT: in case of EMERGENCY to avoid immediate danger; to engage in FISHING within a separation zone

f) [take care near the end of traffic schemes]

g) [avoid anchoring in or near schemes]

h) [give schemes a wide berth]

Overfalls, tide rips, races

i) [fishing vessels must not impede vessels using schemes]
j) *A VESSEL OF LESS THAN 20 METRES OR A SAILING VESSEL shall NOT IMPEDE THE SAFE PASSAGE OF A POWER-DRIVEN VESSEL FOLLOWING A TRAFFIC LANE.*
k) [scheme maintenance vessels may be exempt from this rule]
l) [cable layers may be exempt from this rule]

Section 2 – Conduct of vessels in sight of one another

Rule 11 – Application [Rules apply to vessels in sight of one another]

Rule 12 – Sailing vessels

a) *When two sailing vessels are approaching one another so as to involve the risk of collision, one of them shall keep out of the way of the other as follows:*
   (i)   *when each has the WIND ON A DIFFERENT SIDE, the vessel which has the wind on the PORT SIDE SHALL KEEP OUT OF THE WAY of the other;*
   (ii) *when both have the WIND ON THE SAME SIDE, the vessel which is to WINDWARD SHALL KEEP OUT OF THE WAY of the vessel which is to leeward;*
   (iii) *if a vessel with the wind on the port side sees a vessel to windward and CANNOT DETERMINE WITH CERTAINTY whether the other vessel has the wind on the port or the starboard side, she shall KEEP OUT OF THE WAY of the other.*
b) *For the purposes of this rule the WINDWARD SIDE shall be deemed to be the side OPPOSITE TO that on which the MAINSAIL is carried or, in the case of a square-rigged vessel, the side opposite to that on which the largest fore-and-aft sail is carried.*

Summary – starboard tack has right of way; on the same tack the windward boat gives way; if in doubt keep clear.

Rule 13 – Overtaking

a) Notwithstanding anything contained in the rules ANY VESSEL OVERTAKING any other SHALL KEEP OUT OF THE WAY of the vessel being overtaken.
b) A vessel shall be deemed to be OVERTAKING WHEN coming up with another vessel FROM A DIRECTION MORE THAN 22.5 DEGREES ABAFT HER BEAM, that is, in such a position with reference to the vessel she is overtaking that AT NIGHT she would be ABLE TO SEE ONLY THE STERNLIGHT of that vessel, but neither of her sidelights.
c) When a vessel is in doubt as to whether she is overtaking another, she shall assume that this is the case, and act accordingly.

Note the general principle, also applied in Rules 12 and 14, that if in doubt you keep clear.

d) Any subsequent alteration of the bearing between the two vessels shall not make the overtaking vessel a crossing vessel within the meaning of these rules (ie **Rule 15**), or relieve her of the duty of keeping clear of the overtaken vessel until she is finally past and clear.

Rule 14 – Head-on situation

a) When TWO POWER-DRIVEN VESSELS are MEETING ON RECIPROCAL OR NEARLY RECIPROCAL COURSES so as to involve the risk of collision EACH SHALL ALTER HER COURSE TO STARBOARD so that each shall pass on the port side of the other.

b) Such a situation shall be deemed to exist when a vessel sees the other ahead or nearly ahead and by night she can see the masthead lights of the other in line or nearly in line and/or both sidelights, and by day she observes the corresponding aspect of the other vessel.

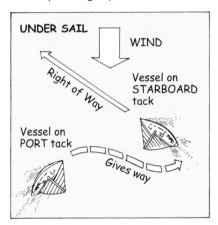

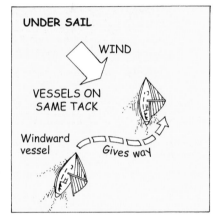

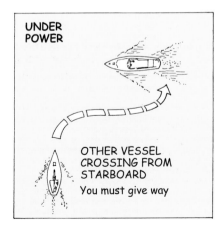

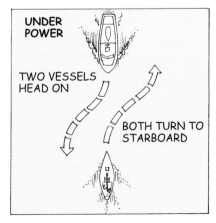

Isolated danger mark

'Hold your course, John, we don't want to confuse him now.'

c) When a vessel is in any doubt as to whether such a situation exists, she shall assume that it does and act accordingly.

Generations of seamen have learnt this rule by memorising Thomas Gray's verses:

> *When you see three lights ahead,*
> *Starboard wheel and show your Red,*
> *Green to Green or Red to Red,*
> *Perfect safety, go ahead.*

Rule 15 – Crossing situation

When TWO POWER-DRIVEN VESSELS are CROSSING so as to involve risk of collision, the VESSEL WHICH HAS THE OTHER ON HER OWN STARBOARD SIDE SHALL KEEP OUT OF THE WAY and shall, if the circumstances of the case admit, avoid crossing ahead of the other vessel.

The Thomas Gray version goes like this:

> *If to your starboard Red appear,*
> *It is your duty to keep clear,*
> *But when upon your port is seen*
> *A steamer's starboard light of Green,*
> *There's not so much for you to do;*
> *The green light must keep clear of you.*

Rule 16 – Action by give-way vessel

Every vessel which is directed to keep out of the way of another vessel shall, so far as possible, TAKE EARLY AND SUBSTANTIAL ACTION to keep well clear.

It does no harm to exaggerate your change of course, to make sure it has been seen.

Rule 17 – Action by stand-on vessel

a) (i) WHERE ONE of two vessels IS TO KEEP OUT OF THE WAY, THE OTHER SHALL KEEP HER COURSE AND SPEED.

(ii) The LATTER MAY HOWEVER TAKE ACTION to avoid collision BY HER MANOEUVRE ALONE AS SOON AS it becomes apparent to her that the VESSEL REQUIRED TO KEEP OUT OF THE WAY IS NOT TAKING APPROPRIATE ACTION in compliance with these rules.

b) When, from any cause, the vessel required to keep her course and speed finds herself so close that collision cannot be avoided by the action of the give-way vessel alone, she shall take such action as will best aid to avoid collision.

Notwithstanding the careful legal wording of (a) and (b), yachtsmen should apply the more basic rule of self preservation.

c) A POWER-DRIVEN VESSEL WHICH TAKES ACTION IN A CROSSING SITUATION in accordance with sub-paragraph (a) (ii) of this rule to avoid collision with another power-driven vessel SHALL, if the circumstances of the case permit, NOT ALTER COURSE TO PORT FOR A VESSEL ON HER OWN PORT SIDE.

d) This rule does not relieve the give-way vessel of her obligation to keep out of the way.

Rule 18 – Responsibilities between vessels

This rule establishes a maritime hierarchy or 'pecking order'. We have printed it in full, but it is probably best learned from the summary given at the end.

Except where Rules 9, 10 and 13 otherwise require –

a) A POWER-DRIVEN VESSEL under way shall KEEP OUT OF THE WAY OF:

(i)   A VESSEL NOT UNDER COMMAND;

(ii) A VESSEL RESTRICTED IN HER ABILITY TO MANOEUVRE;

(iii) A VESSEL ENGAGED IN FISHING;

(iv) A SAILING VESSEL.

b) *A SAILING VESSEL under way shall keep out of the way of:*

(i)   *A VESSEL NOT UNDER COMMAND;*

(ii) *A VESSEL RESTRICTED IN HER ABILITY TO MANOEUVRE;*

(iii) *A VESSEL ENGAGED IN FISHING.*

c) A VESSEL ENGAGED IN FISHING when under way shall, so far as possible, keep out of the way of:

Lighted offshore platform

(i) A VESSEL NOT UNDER COMMAND;
(ii) A VESSEL RESTRICTED IN HER ABILITY TO MANOEUVRE.
d) (i) ANY VESSEL OTHER THAN A VESSEL NOT UNDER COMMAND OR A VESSEL RESTRICTED IN HER ABILITY TO MANOEUVRE shall, if the circumstances of the case admit, AVOID IMPEDING THE SAFE PASSAGE of a VESSEL CONSTRAINED BY HER DRAUGHT, exhibiting the signals in Rule 28

(Three vertical all-round reds or a cylinder.)

(ii) [a vessel constrained by her draught should take special care]
e) [seaplanes should keep well clear]

The maritime 'pecking order'

Vessel not under command.
Vessel restricted in her ability to manoeuvre.
Vessel constrained by her draught.
Fishing vessel – provided she is actually engaged in fishing.
Sailing vessel – but she loses this status when using an auxiliary engine.
Power-driven vessel – she gains status when following a traffic separation lane.
Seaplane – definitely bottom of the pile.
Commercial ships are often big, cumbersome and fast. They can be upon you in less than 10 minutes from appearing over the horizon, yet they may need five or six miles to stop; rapid avoiding action is not usually in their repertoire. For a small yacht or motorboat, therefore, the practical message is to stay clear of her big sisters whenever possible, especially in crowded shipping lanes and harbour entrances – and certainly not rely on the tradition of steam giving way to sail.

Section 3 – Conduct of vessels in restricted visibility

These particular rules are not always fully observed and small sailing craft should not rely on them for protection.

Rule 19

a) [applies to vessels that cannot see one another]
b) EVERY VESSEL SHALL PROCEED AT A SAFE SPEED ADAPTED TO THE PREVAILING CIRCUMSTANCES and conditions of restricted visibility. A power-driven vessel shall have her engines ready for immediate manoeuvre.
c) [take account of poor visibility when following other rules]
d) A vessel which detects by radar alone the presence of another vessel shall determine if a close-quarters situation is developing and/or risk of collision exists. If so, she shall take avoiding action in ample time, provided that

when such action consists of an alteration of course, so far as possible the following shall be avoided:
   (i)   an alteration of course to port for a vessel forward of the beam, other than for a vessel being overtaken;
   (ii)   an alteration of course towards a vessel abeam or abaft the beam.
e) Except where it has been determined that a risk of collision does not exist, every vessel which hears apparently forward of her beam the fog signal of another vessel, or which cannot avoid a close-quarters situation with another vessel forward of her beam, shall reduce her speed to the minimum at which she can be kept on her course. She shall if necessary take all her way off and in any event navigate with extreme caution until danger of collision is over.

PART C – Lights and Shapes

See illustrations in the colour section.

At first sight, the rules on lights and shapes can be bewildering. But don't despair. By logical grouping and elimination – which we have tried to apply in the graphics – they can be made manageable. They are, after all, designed to convey information.

Of the four colours in the basic rules, yellow occurs only rarely. A steady yellow light is confined to tugs, shown above the sternlight to indicate that the vessel is towing. A hovercraft has a flashing yellow light, and a vessel fishing with a seine net may show a pair of alternately flashing yellow lights if she is hampered by her gear. Apart from these few cases – and the lifeboat's blue flashing light – the rules specify combinations of white, red and green.

The first general distinction is between *directional* lights that convey a perspective of movement through the darkness, and *all-round* lights which tell you what kind of vessel you are looking at. A large ship's basic navigation lights, for example, consist of red and green sidelights and a pair of forward-facing white masthead lights, with the rear one set higher than the other so you can tell instantly which way she is heading. But the additional green and white lights shown by a fishing trawler – whether or not she is moving – are visible all round. So are the pilot vessel's white and red lights, or the two reds of a vessel 'not under command'.

Notice that the colour red is generally associated with difficulty or danger – on vessels that are aground, 'manoeuvring with difficulty', 'constrained by their draught', and so on.

Another underlying principle is that you add lights as the vessel – or combination of vessels – gets larger. A small tug on her own may show just a single masthead light, for instance. When towing, the forward light is doubled up, and if the length of the tow exceeds 200 metres, she adds a

Wreck: not dangerous

third. Seen from dead ahead, therefore, she now presents a vertical line of three white lights, plus the red and green sidelights to port and starboard.

- AN IMPORTANT NOTE – to make revision easier, we have summarised the main lights in order of precedence (another 'pecking order') towards the end of this part.

Rule 21 – Definitions

This rule simply defines the visible arc of the various navigation lights – more clearly summarised in our diagram.

Rule 23 – Power-driven vessels under way

a) A POWER-DRIVEN VESSEL UNDER WAY shall exhibit:
 (i)   a MASTHEAD LIGHT forward;
 (ii) a SECOND MASTHEAD LIGHT abaft of and higher than the forward one [this second light is not obligatory for vessels less than 50 metres long];

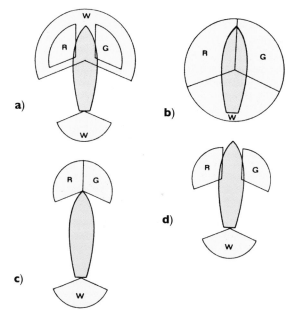

All vessels are required to carry navigation lights between sunset and sunrise apart from very small boats which are only required to carry a torch. In the diagrams R = red, W = white and G = green; a) power-driven vessels, including those with sails and auxiliary engine, carry sidelights, a masthead light and sternlight; b) a sailing vessel of less than 12 metres may carry a tricolour light high on the mast (in place of sidelights and stern-light) c) a sailing boat less than 20 metres may carry a bicolour light and sternlight or d) sidelights and sternlight.

(iii)   SIDELIGHTS;
(iv)   a STERNLIGHT.
b) *An AIR-CUSHION VESSEL when operating in the non-displacement mode shall, in addition to the lights prescribed in paragraph (a) of this rule, exhibit an ALL-ROUND FLASHING YELLOW LIGHT.*
c) (i)   *A POWER-DRIVEN VESSEL OF LESS THAN 12 METRES in length may in lieu of the lights prescribed in paragraph (a) of this rule exhibit an ALL-ROUND WHITE LIGHT AND SIDELIGHTS.*
   (ii)   *A POWER-DRIVEN VESSEL OF LESS THAN 7 METRES in length whose maximum speed does not exceed 7 knots may in lieu of the lights prescribed in paragraph (a) of this rule exhibit an ALL-ROUND WHITE LIGHT and shall, if practicable, also exhibit sidelights.*

Rule 24 – Towing and pushing

a) A POWER-DRIVEN VESSEL WHEN TOWING shall exhibit:
   (i)   instead of the light prescribed in Rule 23a (i)

(The forward masthead light.)

     TWO MASTHEAD LIGHTS FORWARD in a vertical line; WHEN THE LENGTH OF THE TOW, measuring from the stern of the towing vessel to the after end of the tow, EXCEEDS 200 METRES, THREE SUCH LIGHTS in a vertical line;
   (ii)   SIDELIGHTS;
   (iii)   a STERNLIGHT;
   (iv)   a TOWING LIGHT in a vertical line ABOVE THE STERNLIGHT;
   (v)   WHEN THE LENGTH OF THE TOW EXCEEDS 200 METRES, A DIAMOND SHAPE (by day) where it can best be seen.

In other words the characteristics of a tug at night are the extra white masthead lights when seen from ahead and, usually, the yellow towing light seen from astern.

b) [When a pushing vessel and a vessel being pushed ahead are rigidly connected in a composite unit they are regarded as a single power-driven vessel]
c) A POWER-DRIVEN VESSEL WHEN PUSHING AHEAD OR TOWING ALONGSIDE, except in the case of a composite unit, shall exhibit:
   (i)   instead of the light prescribed in Rule 23a (i)

(The forward masthead light.)

     TWO MASTHEAD LIGHTS FORWARD in a vertical line;
   (ii)   SIDELIGHTS;
   (iii)   a STERNLIGHT.

Note the absence of the yellow towing light in this situation.

d) A power-driven vessel to which paragraphs (a) or (c) of this rule apply shall also comply with Rule 23a (ii).

Position from two position circles

(A second masthead light aft in larger vessels.)

e) A VESSEL OR OBJECT BEING TOWED, other than those mentioned in paragraph (g) of the rule shall exhibit:

ie semi-submerged vessel or object

(i)   SIDELIGHTS;
(ii) a STERNLIGHT;
(iii) when the length of the tow exceeds 200 metres, a diamond shape where it can best be seen.

f) [Vessels being towed alongside or pushed, but not in a composite unit, need their own sidelights and, if alongside, a sternlight]

g) An inconspicuous partly submerged vessel or object, or combination of such vessels or objects being towed, shall exhibit: [multiple all-round white lights and diamonds to indicate their size].

h) [if impracticable to light a tow properly, 'all possible measures' must be taken at least to indicate its presence]

(eg by illuminating it with a searchlight.)

Rule 25 – Sailing vessels under way and vessels under oars

a) *A SAILING VESSEL UNDER WAY shall exhibit:*
   (i)   *SIDELIGHTS;*
   (ii) *a STERNLIGHT;*

b) *In a SAILING VESSEL OF LESS THAN 12 METRES in length the LIGHTS prescribed in paragraph (a) of this rule MAY BE COMBINED IN ONE LANTERN carried at or near the top of the mast where it can best be seen.*

c) *A SAILING VESSEL under way may, IN ADDITION to the lights prescribed in paragraph (a) of this rule*

(Sidelights and sternlight)

exhibit at or near the top of the mast... TWO ALL-ROUND LIGHTS in a vertical line, THE UPPER BEING RED AND THE LOWER GREEN, but these lights shall not be exhibited in conjunction with the combined lantern permitted by paragraph (b) of this rule.

d) *A SAILING VESSEL OF LESS THAN 7 METRES in length shall, if practicable, exhibit the lights prescribed in paragraph (a) or (b) of this rule, but if she does not, she shall have ready at hand AN ELECTRIC TORCH OR LIGHTED LANTERN showing a white light which shall be exhibited in sufficient time to prevent collision. [The same applies to a VESSEL UNDER OARS.]*

e) *A VESSEL PROCEEDING UNDER SAIL (in daylight) WHEN ALSO BEING PROPELLED BY MACHINERY shall exhibit forward where it can best be seen A CONICAL SHAPE DOWNWARDS.*

A rule rarely obeyed in British waters.

Rule 26 – Fishing vessels

a) A vessel engaged in fishing, whether under way or at anchor, shall exhibit only the lights and shapes prescribed in this rule.

Wishful thinking!

b) A VESSEL ENGAGED IN TRAWLING... shall exhibit:
  (i)   TWO ALL-ROUND LIGHTS in a vertical line, THE UPPER BEING GREEN AND THE OTHER WHITE [or by day, two cones one above the other, with their apexes together]

Like the topmark of a westerly cardinal buoy.

  (ii) [the normal masthead light or lights]
  (iii) [when making way through the water, the normal sidelights and sternlight]

So a single green, all-round light means it is a trawler (though a dredger and a minesweeper may show two or three green lights respectively) whereas other fishing vessels – see below – show all-round red over white.

c) A VESSEL ENGAGED IN FISHING OTHER THAN TRAWLING shall exhibit:
  (i)   TWO ALL-ROUND LIGHTS in a vertical line, THE UPPER BEING RED AND THE LOWER WHITE [or by day, two cones, apexes together];
  (ii) When there is OUTLYING GEAR extending more than 150 metres horizontally from the vessel. An ALL-ROUND WHITE LIGHT OR A CONE APEX UPWARDS IN THE DIRECTION OF THE GEAR;
  (iii) [when making way through the water, normal sidelights and sternlight]

[Annex II prescribes extra light signals for trawlers: TWO VERTICAL WHITE LIGHTS when SHOOTING their nets, WHITE OVER RED when HAULING nets, and TWO VERTICAL REDS when NETS FAST on an obstruction; TRAWLERS FISHING IN PAIRS may direct SEARCHLIGHTS at each other.

The Annex also prescribes signals for purse seiners: TWO VERTICAL YELLOW LIGHTS, FLASHING ALTERNATELY every second, but only when the vessel is hampered by her gear]

Rule 27 – Vessels not under command or restricted in their ability to manoeuvre

a) A VESSEL NOT UNDER COMMAND

(NUC for short)

shall exhibit:
  (i)   TWO ALL-ROUND RED LIGHTS in a vertical line;
  (ii) TWO BALLS (by day) or similar shapes in a vertical line;
  (iii) [in addition, when making way through the water, normal sidelights and sternlight]

b) A VESSEL RESTRICTED IN HER ABILITY TO MANOEUVRE

(Known as RAM)

shall exhibit:

West cardinal buoy

(i) THREE ALL-ROUND LIGHTS in a vertical line [RED, WHITE, RED];
(ii) THREE SHAPES (by day) in a vertical line [BALL, DIAMOND, BALL];
(iii) [in addition, when making way through the water, normal masthead light or lights, sidelights and sternlight]
(iv) When AT ANCHOR [at least one all-round white light or ball, in addition to red/white/red or equivalent shapes];
c) [A power-driven vessel hampered by towing should show a tug's lights and those of a vessel restricted in her ability to manoeuvre]
d) A VESSEL ENGAGED IN DREDGING or underwater operations, when restricted in her ability to manoeuvre, shall exhibit the lights and shapes prescribed in this rule and, in addition, when an obstruction exists:
(i) TWO ALL-ROUND RED LIGHTS OR TWO BALLS in a vertical line TO INDICATE the side on which the OBSTRUCTION exists;
(ii) TWO ALL-ROUND GREEN LIGHTS OR TWO DIAMONDS in a vertical line TO INDICATE the side on which another VESSEL MAY PASS;
(iii) [at anchor this rule still applies, not Rule 30]
e) [Small vessels engaged in diving operations may show three all-round lights – red, white, red – and a rigid replica of the international code flag 'A']
f) A VESSEL ENGAGED IN MINE CLEARANCE OPERATIONS shall, in addition to the lights prescribed in Rules 23 and 30, exhibit THREE ALL-ROUND GREEN LIGHTS OR THREE BALLS; one of these lights or shapes shall be exhibited near the foremasthead and one at each end of the fore yard. These lights or shapes indicate that it is DANGEROUS for another vessel TO APPROACH WITHIN 1000 METRES...
g) *[vessels of less than 12 metres need not comply unless engaged in diving operations]*

Rule 28 – Vessels constrained by their draught
A VESSEL CONSTRAINED BY HER DRAUGHT

(CBD for short)

may, in addition to the lights prescribed for power-driven vessels in Rule 23, exhibit where they can best be seen THREE ALL-ROUND RED LIGHTS in a vertical line OR A CYLINDER.

Signalling the order of precedence

NUC	Two vertical reds or two balls
RAM	Three vertical red/white/red or ball/diamond/ball
CBD	Three vertical reds or a cylinder
Fishing	Green over white or red over white, or twin cones
Sailing	Red over green or combined red and green
Power	White all-round or masthead white

+

Rule 29 – Pilot vessels

a) A VESSEL ENGAGED ON PILOTAGE DUTY shall exhibit:
   (i)   at or near the masthead, TWO ALL-ROUND LIGHTS in a vertical line, the UPPER BEING WHITE AND THE LOWER RED

The same colours as some fishing vessels, but the order reversed

   (ii)   [when under way, normal sidelights and sternlight]
   (iii) [when at anchor, in addition, the lights or shapes prescribed in Rule 30 below]

Rule 30 – Anchored vessels and vessels aground

a) A VESSEL AT ANCHOR shall exhibit where it can best be seen:
   (i)   IN THE FORE PART, an ALL-ROUND WHITE LIGHT OR ONE BALL;
   (ii)   at or NEAR THE STERN AND AT A LOWER LEVEL than the light pre-scribed in sub-paragraph (i), an ALL-ROUND WHITE LIGHT.
b) *A VESSEL OF LESS THAN 50 METRES in length may exhibit an ALL-ROUND WHITE LIGHT instead of the lights prescribed in paragraph (a).*
c) [Large vessels at anchor must switch on their deck lights]
d) A VESSEL AGROUND shall exhibit the lights prescribed in paragraph (a) or (b) of this rule and IN ADDITION, where they can best be seen:
   (i)   TWO ALL-ROUND RED LIGHTS in a vertical line;
   (ii)   THREE BALLS in a vertical line.
e) *A VESSEL OF LESS THAN 7 METRES in length, when AT ANCHOR NOT IN OR NEAR A NARROW CHANNEL, FAIRWAY OR ANCHORAGE, or where other vessels normally navigate [need not comply with this rule];*
f) *A VESSEL OF LESS THAN 12 METRES in length, WHEN AGROUND [need not comply with this rule].*

In spite of the immense care taken when drafting the colregs, lights can still occasionally be confusing or ambiguous. Consider the simplest example – a single white light. In an exam question, it could represent several things – sternlight, anchor light, small powerboat under way. At sea, the context may make things clear (the powerboat will move, whereas the anchor light will not), but against an array of shore lights, the single white can easily go unnoticed or unrecognised. In the same way, ships whose decks are typically ablaze with working lights – fishing vessels, warships, ferries – are notoriously confusing. Whereas the twin masthead lights and sidelights of a darkened freighter instantly convey her relative movement.

Rule 31– Seaplanes

Dead reckoning position

PART D - Sound and Light Signals

Rule 32 - Definitions

b) ['short blast' means about 1 second]
c) ['prolonged blast' means 4–6 seconds]

Rule 33 - Equipment for sound signals

a) A VESSEL OF 12 METRES OR MORE in length shall be provided with a WHISTLE AND A BELL, and a VESSEL OF 100 METRES OR MORE in length shall, IN ADDITION, be provided with a GONG.
b) *A VESSEL OF LESS THAN 12 METRES in length [need not carry a whistle, bell or gong, but if so she must have some other efficient means of sounding a signal].*

Rule 34 - Manoeuvring and warning signals

a) When vessels are in sight of one another, a POWER-DRIVEN VESSEL UNDER WAY, when manoeuvring… shall indicate that manoeuvre by the following signals on her whistle:
ONE SHORT BLAST – 'I AM ALTERING MY COURSE TO STARBOARD'
TWO SHORT BLASTS – 'I AM ALTERING MY COURSE TO PORT'
THREE SHORT BLASTS – 'I AM OPRERATING ASTERN PROPULSION'
b) any vessel may supplement the whistle signals prescribed in this rule by light signals:
one flash – 'I am altering my course to starboard'
two flashes – 'I am altering my course to port'
three flashes – 'I am operating astern propulsion'
[ie one-second white all-round flashes]
c) When in sight of one another in a narrow channel or fairway:
(i)   a VESSEL INTENDING TO OVERTAKE another shall in compliance with Rule 9e (i) indicate her intention by the following signals on her whistle:
TWO PROLONGED BLASTS FOLLOWED BY ONE SHORT – 'I INTEND TO OVERTAKE YOU ON YOUR STARBOARD SIDE'
TWO PROLONGED BLASTS FOLLOWED BY TWO SHORT – 'I INTEND TO OVERTAKE YOU ON YOUR PORT SIDE'
(ii)   the VESSEL ABOUT TO BE OVERTAKEN when acting in accordance with Rule 9e (i) shall INDICATE AGREEMENT by ONE PROLONGED, ONE SHORT, ONE PROLONGED AND ONE SHORT BLAST
d) When vessels in sight of one another are approaching each other and from any cause either VESSEL FAILS TO UNDERSTAND THE INTENTIONS OR ACTIONS of the other, OR IS IN DOUBT WHETHER SUFFICIENT ACTION IS BEING TAKEN by the other TO AVOID COLLISION, the vessel in doubt shall

● ● ● ▬ ▬ ▬ ● ● ●

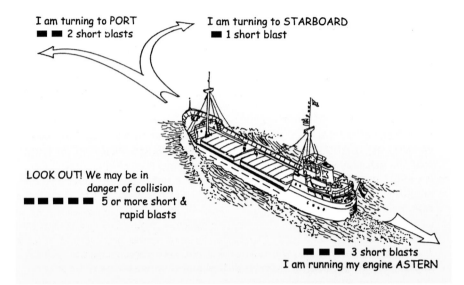

I am turning to PORT
■ ■ 2 short blasts

I am turning to STARBOARD
■ 1 short blast

LOOK OUT! We may be in
danger of collision
■ ■ ■ ■ ■ 5 or more short &
rapid blasts

■ ■ ■ 3 short blasts
I am running my engine ASTERN

immediately indicate such doubt by giving at least FIVE SHORT AND RAPID BLASTS on the whistle [plus five short flashes if appropriate].

An important signal calculated to strike fear into the heart of any yachtsman.

e) A VESSEL NEARING A BEND or an area of a channel or fairway where other vessels may be obscured by an intervening obstruction shall sound ONE PROLONGED BLAST. Such signal shall be ANSWERED WITH A PROLONGED BLAST...

Rule 35 – Sound signals in restricted visibility

In or near an area of restricted visibility, whether by day or night:

a) A POWER-DRIVEN VESSEL MAKING WAY THROUGH THE WATER shall sound, at intervals of not more than 2 minutes, ONE PROLONGED BLAST.

b) A POWER-DRIVEN VESSEL UNDER WAY BUT STOPPED and making no way through the water shall sound, at intervals of not more than 2 minutes, TWO PROLONGED BLASTS.

c) A vessel NOT UNDER COMMAND, a vessel RESTRICTED IN HER ABILITY TO MANOEUVRE, a vessel CONSTRAINED BY HER DRAUGHT, a SAILING vessel, a vessel ENGAGED IN FISHING and a vessel ENGAGED IN TOWING OR PUSHING another vessel shall, instead of the signals prescribed in paragraphs (a) or (b) of this rule, sound at intervals of not more than 2 minutes, three blasts in succession, namely ONE PROLONGED FOLLOWED BY TWO SHORT BLASTS.

d) [Rule 35c) above also applies to anchored fishing vessels and vessels whose work hampers their ability to manoeuvre]

SOS

e) A VESSEL TOWED shall at intervals of not more than 2 minutes sound ONE PROLONGED FOLLOWED BY THREE SHORT BLASTS.

f) [pushing tug and pushed vessel if rigidly connected are regarded as single power-driven vessel]

g) A VESSEL AT ANCHOR shall AT INTERVALS OF NOT MORE THAN ONE MINUTE RING THE BELL RAPIDLY for about 5 seconds. In a VESSEL OF 100 METRES OR MORE in length the BELL SHALL BE SOUNDED IN THE FORE PART of the vessel AND IMMEDIATELY AFTER the ringing of the bell the GONG shall be SOUNDED RAPIDLY for about 5 seconds IN THE AFTER PART of the vessel. A vessel at anchor MAY IN ADDITION sound three blasts in succession, namely ONE SHORT, ONE PROLONGED AND ONE SHORT BLAST, to give warning...

h) A VESSEL AGROUND shall give the bell signal and if required the gong signal prescribed, and IN ADDITION, give THREE SEPARATE AND DISTINCT STROKES ON THE BELL IMMEDIATELY BEFORE AND AFTER THE RAPID RINGING of the bell. A vessel aground may in addition sound an appropriate whistle signal.

i) *A VESSEL OF LESS THAN 12 METRES in length [need not give the above signals, but must make some other effective signal every two minutes].*

j) [A pilot vessel may sound four short blasts]

PEYTON

'They want to know if we've got the East Sunk on board.'

Ropework

Modern synthetic ropes (as opposed to those made from natural fibres like hemp) come in **two main forms**, using one of **three materials**.

Some are **laid** or **twisted** from three strands, making them easy to splice together, for example to form a loop; others are **plaited** or **braided** from many strands, which makes for a more flexible rope, easy to tie and less liable to kinks.

The three main materials are:

- **Nylon**, which stretches to absorb loads, and is therefore good for anchor warps and some mooring lines;
- **Polyester** (eg Terylene), which does not stretch much, making it more suitable for sail halyards and most other purposes;
- **Polypropylene**, a cheaper floating material, which makes a good rescue line and maybe a dinghy towing painter, but not much else.

There are many other specialised or composite ropes, some using aramid (eg Kevlar), an extremely strong but expensive material.

The shorebased Day Skipper syllabus no longer includes practical ropework – how to tie knots, use a winch, stow a coil and so on – but you will of course need to acquire this knowledge as soon as you step on board a boat, or embark on one of the RYA's practical courses. So while you are learning the nautical terms, look out for these knots and hitches:

Eight essential knots

- The simple **round turn and two half hitches**, that will tie a rope to a mooring ring or a post, and will not jam under tension.
- The **clove hitch**: good for suspending fenders from a guard rail, often tied with a quick-release loop.
- Its useful derivative, the **rolling hitch**, with an extra jamming turn which prevents it sliding in that direction.
- The **reef knot**, excellent when reefing a sail, but useless for tying two ropes together.
- The **sheet bend**, and **double sheet bend**, which *will* quickly join two ropes.

Dangerous underwater wreck

- The **figure of eight stopper** knot, for the ends of sheets.
- The **bowline**, the archetypal sailor's knot – best learnt, not by following rabbits round trees, but as a series of hand movements, because this way it is just as easy to tie in the dark, or without looking; it is difficult to jam and has a hundred and one uses, such as dropping the end of a mooring line over a bollard.

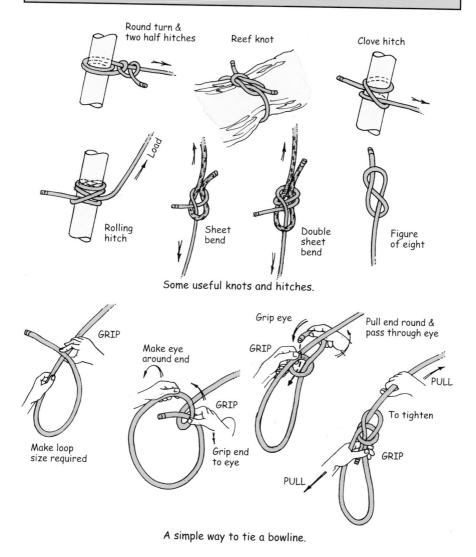

Round turn & two half hitches

Reef knot

Clove hitch

Rolling hitch

Sheet bend

Double sheet bend

Figure of eight

Load

Some useful knots and hitches.

GRIP

Make loop size required

Make eye around end

GRIP

Grip end to eye

PULL

Grip eye

GRIP

Pull end round & pass through eye

PULL

To tighten

PULL

GRIP

A simple way to tie a bowline.

Down at the harbour, notice the way boats are moored – not just with bow and stern lines, but also with criss-crossed 'springs' to prevent any fore and aft movement. On board, get someone to demonstrate the winches and how to sheet in a headsail – one turn to take in the slack and usually two more turns to provide enough friction for hardening in, while watching out for the dreaded 'riding turn'.

Points to remember about ropework

- Don't hesitate to use a final locking turn when cleating off any modern synthetic rope which cannot be allowed to come loose – such as a dinghy painter. The residual prejudice against this habit goes back to the days of natural fibres, which tended to jam solid when they became wet.
- Almost every rope retains some inherent twist – and hence a maddening tendency to tangle. Paradoxically, the way to make a coil of rope lie flat and ready to run clear is to put a twist into each loop as you pass it into the coiling hand. Finish with several tight horizontal turns, loop the last of them through and back over the top of the coil, then pull tight. Finally, hang the coil or lay it carefully in a locker with the tail ready to grab. A tangled rope is worse than useless in an emergency.

Visitors' moorings

Safety

Sailing can never be made absolutely safe, and if it were, it would lose much of its appeal. So where safety equipment and practice are concerned, there are many different views on what constitutes a reasonable compromise. But for exam purposes, err on the side of caution and your instructor's guidance. The standards suggested here are mainly based on RYA/DoT recommendations (the relevant RYA booklet is C8).

SOLAS

The **Maritime and Coastguard Agency (MCA)** has adopted new International Maritime Organisation regulations known as the Convention for the Safety of Life at Sea (**SOLAS**). In the summer of 2002 these were applied to recreational craft. There are certain mandatory requirements which include:

- A passage plan must be prepared for voyages outside Categorised Waters (normally estuaries and harbours).
- All vessels are to carry a suitable radar reflector.
- An illustrated table describing the life-saving signals shall be readily available on board.
- Skippers are required to respond to distress messages from any source.
- The misuse of distress signals is prohibited.
- Skippers must report any unmarked hazards.

More information is available from the RYA on their website at www.rya.org.uk.

Safety equipment

Everyone on board should have some sort of **lifejacket**. A proper lifejacket, as opposed to a **buoyancy aid**, is designed to turn an unconscious person on to his back and support his head above water. However the advantage of some buoyancy aids – those that double as oilskins or windproof waistcoats for example – is that you are more likely to be wearing them when you fall overboard.

The old sailor's rule about 'one hand for the ship, the other for yourself' makes perfect sense on a small yacht. Even better is a **safety harness** running on

2 vertical red lights

a suitable jackstay along the deck. You should carry at least enough harnesses to equip the watch on deck in bad weather and at night (the DoT recommends one for each person on board). When attaching a lifeline to the boat, beware the size of U bolt that will prise the spring hook open – or use a locking hook.

A yacht should carry at least two **lifebuoys** for throwing to a man overboard (buoyant cushions also throw well) with a long floating line if appropriate. At night, an **automatic light** attached to the lifebuoy (the light only comes on when it inverts in a floating position) could be a lifesaver. And the same goes for reflective patches on waterproof clothing. Even during the day, keeping continuous watch on the casualty overboard is a vital aspect of the man-overboard drill; it is much easier if you can drop a tall **dan buoy** like those fishermen use to mark crab pots and nets.

Radar reflectors

Big ships should maintain a radar watch as well as a visual lookout, and the MCA guidance is that all boats should hoist a suitably-sized **radar reflector**, as high as possible to aid detection by ships. The basic type consists of aluminium plates slotted together in a shape known as an octahedral, fixed so it presents one of its hollow reflective corners to the radar transmitter's beam (and 'catches water' in the upper corner). More efficient for their size (that is producing a bigger blip on the ship's radar screen) are reflectors that encapsulate a number of hollow metal shapes in a plastic casing, which then hoists naturally in the correct position.

Radio distress calls

In most situations requiring flares, a vessel equipped with **VHF (Very High Frequency) radio** would already have put out a **distress call** or 'Mayday' (from the French *m'aidez*).

VHF is a line-of-sight system with a range of 30–40 miles when talking to a coastal station like the Coastguard and perhaps 10 miles when calling another yacht. Handheld VHF sets, looking like mobile phones, have a smaller range still, because of their limited power.

There are various designated frequencies, or 'channels'. Calls usually start on **channel 16** – which is also the **international distress frequency** – before switching quickly to a working channel. The full operating procedure, using the characteristic word 'over', spelling with a phonetic alphabet (see below) and so on, is explained in the RYA pamphlet G 22. The Day Skipper course only covers distress calls.

A Mayday call should only be made when you or your yacht are 'in grave and imminent danger' and require 'immediate assistance'. In that case, this is the procedure:

Vessel not under command

'An unmarked wreck? It's about a billion to one chance.'

Making a Mayday call: select channel 16 at high power, and speaking slowly and clearly, transmit:

- MAYDAY, MAYDAY, MAYDAY
- THIS IS (name of yacht, repeated three times)
- MAYDAY (name of yacht, spoken once)
- MY POSITION IS (Lat and Long, or true bearing and distance from charted mark)
- I AM (sinking, on fire, or whatever)
- I HAVE (number of persons on board who are eg taking to a liferaft and/or firing distress rockets)
- I REQUIRE IMMEDIATE ASSISTANCE
- OVER

The Phonetic Alphabet

A – Alpha	B – Bravo	C – Charlie
D – Delta	E – Echo	F – Foxtrot
G – Golf	H – Hotel	I – India
J – Juliet	K – Kilo	L – Lima
M – Mike	N – November	O – Oscar
P – Papa	Q – Quebec	R – Romeo
S – Sierra	T – Tango	U – Uniform
V – Victor	W – Whiskey	X – X-ray
Y – Yankee	Z – Zulu	

GMDSS

Using the **Global Maritime Distress and Safety System (GMDSS)**, you can transmit the first part of this call (that is the Mayday, the yacht's identity and position) automatically, using a digital attachment known as a **Digital Selective Calling (DSC)** controller. Each controller is programmed with a unique nine-digit number – the **Maritime Mobile Service Identity (MMSI) number** – which acts rather like a telephone number, rather than a name, to identify the vessel. A Coastguard station therefore knows who is in trouble, and if the DSC controller is linked to a GPS unit – as the GMDSS assumes – the station also receives the vessel's position (alternatively, the controller can be manually programmed with the latest position and its time). The person needing assistance waits 15 seconds for an automatic acknowledgment from the Coastguard, or a ship, before repeating the distress call by voice on channel 16.

The type of controller designed for small yachts cannot automatically acknowledge a DSC distress call from someone else. So once it seems clear that a

Occulting light (Oc) – light periods exceed dark

call has not been heard elsewhere, the message should be 'relayed' on channel 16, preceded by the words 'MAYDAY RELAY, MAYDAY RELAY, MAYDAY RELAY'.

For the foreseeable future, **GMDSS will only be compulsory for merchant ships** of more than 300 gross tonnes. Yachts can carry on with the basic VHF system, but are warned that from February 2005, the Coastguard ceased to maintain a dedicated 'headset' distress watch on channel 16. Stations still, however, monitor channel 16 on a loudspeaker in operations rooms.

Another form of automatic distress signal under the GMDSS umbrella is an **Emergency Position Indicating Radio Beacon (EPIRB)** which uses satellites to alert the rescue services.

There are many situations falling short of 'grave and imminent danger' when help is nevertheless urgently needed, or nearby shipping needs to be informed. A yacht might be drifting across a shipping lane with a broken mast or a fouled propeller. Or there might be a serious medical emergency on board.

In such cases, an **'urgency' radio signal** should be made to 'ALL STATIONS', preceded by the words 'PAN-PAN, PAN-PAN, PAN-PAN', giving the yacht's name and position, followed by a brief explanation of the problem.

'My position? On top of the doghouse.'

Essential points to remember – calling for assistance

You can use:
- Red hand flare or rocket
- Orange smoke flare
- 'MAYDAY' VHF radio distress call
- EPIRB
- SOS Morse code signal (...---...) by any means
- International code letter V by Morse (...-) or flag, meaning - 'I require assistance'
- International code flags NC (each flag represents a letter, as well as having its own meaning)
- Square flag with a ball over or under it
- Continuous sounding of foghorn
- Continuous raising and lowering of the arms

Abandoning ship

Should you have to pick somebody up (the recommended techniques for this are covered in the Day Skipper practical course), it will probably help immensely to have a deep **boarding ladder** over the side.

Offshore, you may need an automatically inflating **liferaft**, but don't be tempted to abandon the yacht unless it is sinking fast or on fire – crews have been lost in this way while their abandoned boat stayed afloat.

A **rescue helicopter**, on the other hand, may instruct you to take to the water – in a dinghy at the end of a long warp, or just wearing your lifejacket – to make winching you up easier. Points to note:

- The winching wire will be preceded by a light line to guide it down (let the wire touch the water before handling it, to discharge static electricity).
- If a winchman comes down to take charge, he will probably land on the port quarter.
- Clear the decks as far as possible of anything that might snag the wire – *and never make it fast.*
- The lifting strop goes under your armpits and tightens with a toggle – keep your arms down, even though this feels unnatural.
- If radio communication is possible, it will almost certainly be on channel 16.

Special mark

When you know that a lifeboat or a helicopter is nearby and searching for you, the best way to direct it may be to use a distress flare (but not, of course, where the flare could endanger the helicopter).

Distress flares

These come in various forms – orange smoke signals (visible on a clear day up to about 3 miles); red hand flares (visible up to about 10 miles at night in clear visibility); red parachute rockets (visible at more than 20 miles unless fired into low cloud).

The minimum recommended combination depends on a yacht's cruising range:

- **Inshore** (sheltered waters such as an estuary) – **2 hand flares, 2 orange smokes.**
- **Coastal** (up to 10 miles from land) – **2 parachute rockets, 2 hand flares, 2 orange smokes.**
- **Offshore** (more than 10 miles from land) – **4 parachute rockets, 4 hand flares, 2 buoyant orange smokes.**

Many skippers also like to carry **white hand flares** as a 'deterrent' to ships on a collision course at night. A few yachts carry a Very pistol which fires small flares.

As a last resort, a **powerful waterproof torch** is obviously better than nothing. In fact it is good practice to have two torches – one for everyday use, the other handy for real emergencies.

Maritime and Coastguard Agency (MCA)

If you ever use these distress signals, it will probably be the Coastguard that send a lifeboat or helicopter to your rescue. Founded in 1822 to control smuggling, the service (Maritime and Coastguard Agency (MCA) since 1998) now operates through a chain of coastal rescue centres, manned 24 hours a day and equipped with powerful radio communications. They also issue weather forecasts.

Fire and explosions on board

Fire is more dangerous at sea than on land, even though you are surrounded by water. Any yacht with either cooking equipment or an engine (especially a petrol engine) needs at least one fire extinguisher. The recommended equipment for smaller yachts is **two 1.5-kilogram dry powder extinguishers** (carbon dioxide or foam are alternatives, but powder is what the fire brigade use for their own vehicles). Large motor yachts should have an automatic extinguisher built into the engine compartment.

A **fire blanket** is the best way to smother fires, for example in the galley. And of course sea water may do the job, provided you are not dealing with spilt engine fuel. In any case, every boat needs at least one **bucket** on a lanyard, and a flat **bailer** for the dinghy.

Far worse than a simple fire is the danger of exploding petrol fumes or cooking gas. This type of gas is heavier than air, so if it does escape it tends to collect in the bilges – which is why gas bottles should be stored in a special locker that drains overboard. The most important precaution is closing the valve on the bottle whenever it is not needed. Some boats carry gas detectors. If there is a leak into the bilges, a diaphragm pump will help clear them.

Two **pumps**, easy to dismantle and workable from secure positions, are in any case a basic piece of safety equipment. One of them could be an electric pump, that will keep going when you and your crew tire.

First aid

The boat's **first aid kit** should include bandages, dressings for burns, antiseptic, painkillers and seasickness tablets. But another most important item is a book on first aid which includes instructions for giving mouth-to-mouth resuscitation and ways of treating hypothermia – because not knowing what to do for the best can aggravate an injury as well as alarming those involved. Remember that the *Reeds Nautical Almanac* has a useful first aid section.

Safety equipment checklist

- Lifejackets – one for each crew member
- Safety harnesses – one for each crew member
- Lifebuoys – two
- Dan buoy
- Buoyant automatic light
- Boarding ladder
- Liferaft – inflated inflatable, or rigid dinghy with lots of built-in buoyancy, are both viable options
- Flares – four red parachutes, four red hand-held flares, two buoyant orange smokes, two white flares
- Fire extinguishers – two 1.5 kilogram dry powder or equivalent
- Fire blanket
- First aid kit
- Waterproof torch and spare batteries
- Radar reflector
- Foghorn
- Bilge pumps – two
- Bucket and bailer

Tidal stream

'Just keep her jogging along while I have a recap.'

Communications

Maritime communications have evolved over centuries, from the signal flags to which Nelson turned a blind eye, through semaphore, Morse telegraphy and the Aldis lamp, to various forms of radio. Modern systems make extensive use of satellites and of course the **VHF radiotelephones** and **DSC** we discussed under the heading 'Safety'.

But elements of the older methods remain, and can still be useful in certain situations. As we saw earlier, the Morse code SOS (...---...) is still a universally recognised signal of distress, along with the Mayday radio call. Many yachts fly a red or blue national ensign at the stern even in home waters (the white ensign is confined to the Royal Navy and the Royal Yacht Squadron) and you will notice that as a courtesy, visiting foreign yachts fly our ensign at their starboard crosstrees. If you see a yellow 'Q' flag, it is there to inform Customs that the yacht has returned directly from a port outside the EU (or from the Channel Islands).

The humble **mobile phone** is sometimes scorned or ignored by maritime authorities because it is evidently not a substitute for a VHF marine radio. Yet within its limited range, it offers another valuable way of contacting the emergency services ashore and has certainly saved lives. So if you have one, always take it aboard!

Environmental awareness

Increasing public concern about protecting our environment extends to the sea, and hence to yachtsmen. Four basic principles are endorsed by the RYA:

- **Garbage** – do not dump it at sea, but retain for disposal ashore
- **Oily wastes** – prevent any discharge of oil, fuel or similar harmful substances
- **Sewage** – do not discharge a sea toilet where it affects water quality or amenity
- **Toxic wastes** – keep toxic or damaging chemicals (such as antifouling) out of the sea

So that's it, Skipper! Best of luck with those exams, and good sailing!

South cardinal buoy

Index